Series/Number 07-027

DYNAMIC MODELING
An Introduction

R. ROBERT HUCKFELDT
University of Notre Dame

C. W. KOHFELD
University of Missouri-St. Louis

THOMAS W. LIKENS
Anheuser-Busch Companies

SAGE PUBLICATIONS
The International Professional Publishers
Newbury Park   London   New Delhi

For information address:

 SAGE Publications, Inc.
2455 Teller Road
Newbury Park, California 91320
E-mail: order@sagepub.com

1 Olivers Yard, 55 City Road
London EC1Y 1SP

SAGE Publications India Pvt Ltd
B-42 Panchsheel Enclave
PO Box 4109
New Dehli 110 017

Printed in the United States of America

International Standard Book Number 0-8039-0946-2

Library of Congress Catalog Card No. L.C. 82-0426101

03 04 10

When citing a university paper, please use the proper form. Remember to cite the Sage University Paper series title and include the paper number. One of the following formats can be adapted (depending on the style manual used):

(1) HENKEL, RAMON E. (1976) Tests of Significance. Sage University Paper Series on Quantitative Applications in the Social Sciences, 07-004. Newbury Park, CA: Sage.

OR

(2) Henkel, R. E. (1976). *Tests of significance* (Sage University Paper Series on Quantitative Applications in the Social Sciences, series no. 07-04). Newbury Park, CA: Sage.

CONTENTS

Series Editor's Introduction

R. Robert Huckfeldt, C. W. Kohfeld, and Thomas W. Likens have added a new dimension to this series by writing *Dynamic Modeling: An Introduction*. In this monograph, they introduce the reader to the tools necessary for sophisticated modeling of the processes of social change, broadly understood. Their emphasis is on the use of difference equations in modeling such changes, although their treatment of the topic is such that no advanced training in mathematics is required. Unlike differential equation models, in which time is treated as continuous and rates of change are considered to be instantaneous, in difference equation models, time is treated as a series of discrete, equally spaced units. The latter have probably been given less attention by social scientists, but in many instances, such models often make more substantive sense.

Using examples that include models of social and political mobilization, diffusion, and social interaction, Huckfeldt et al. introduce the reader to first-order linear and nonlinear difference equation models in Chapters 2 and 3. They show the novice how to examine the conditions of equilibrium and stability, and how to estimate the parameters of each model. Examples abound, simplifying the presentation and assisting the mathematically untrained reader in his or her attempt to understand the application of difference equation models in the social sciences.

In Chapters 4 and 5, the authors move beyond first-order equations, discussing linear and nonlinear higher-order equations in the two chapters, respectively. There is an extended example of arms race models, developed by Richardson and expanded upon by Gillespie and Zinnes in recent years, as well as modeling examples of legislative review and of the budgetary process.

With exception of Chapter 5, the authors have presented this reasonably complex material without assuming much more than high school algebra. The mathematics developed in Chapters 5, on nonlinear dynamic systems, is more demanding but the authors' intention "is not to equip readers fully with the analytical methods required to conduct similar analyses, but rather to illustrate the direction in which the work in this monograph naturally moves." The extended example of budgetary competition is therefore meant as illustrative and should not be beyond the reach of most of our readers when they read it within the framework of the authors' intentions.

Most of the previous monographs published in this series have been purely statistical in orientation. This monograph is an introduction to mathematical modeling and as such represents the first in a series of departures from that theme. The Quantitative Applications series will shortly publish monographs on nonstatistical topics such as questionnaire design and construction. As the topics covered by this series broaden, our intentions remain firm: to present simple, readable introductions to topics of interest to social scientists who engage primarily in quantitative work.

—*John L. Sullivan*
Series Co-Editor

ACKNOWLEDGMENTS

The effort in these pages is dedicated to our teacher: John Sprague of Washington University. For all three of us he has been a dissertation chairman, a continuing source of sound advice, and a good friend.

A number of other colleagues have provided valuable encouragement and advice as well. We especially wish to thank Ronald Weber of Louisiana State University, who initially helped us formulate the project, and several anonymous reviewers who provided some very helpful and constructive criticisms.

Finally, the federal government has been by our side, rather than on our back, throughout this project. Kohfeld and Likens were supported under NSF grant SOC79-09308 made to the University of Kentucky. Huckfeldt was supported under NSF grant SES80-14231 made to Louisiana State University, and NSF grant SES81-18597 made to the University of Notre Dame.

This project has been fully and equally shared among the three authors. Credit or blame is equally shared as well. We considered several different randomization procedures for ordering the authors' names, but Huckfeldt thought that alphabetical order might be best.

DYNAMIC MODELING

An Introduction

R. ROBERT HUCKFELDT
University of Notre Dame

C. W. KOHFELD
University of Missouri—St. Louis

THOMAS W. LIKENS
Anheuser-Busch Companies

1. DYNAMIC MODELS AND SOCIAL CHANGE

Social reality is more than a set of substantively related but randomly occurring events. In this monograph we think of social phenomena as processes—structured series of events, operations, and activities whose logic is orderly and predictable. The goal of dynamic modeling is to specify the structure of such processes and to deduce the manner in which they generate social change.

This monograph presents a set of techniques and strategies for dynamic modeling within the context of several substantive applications. One component demonstrates the translation of substantive ideas into precise, mathematical statements. We are concerned with a technology for specifying models that have (1) mathematically based substantive interpretations, and (2) logically tractable and meaningful deductive consequences. Indeed, descriptive adequacy—a persuasive descriptive interpretation for a model and its consequences—is the main technical criterion for model evaluation.

Difference Equations as Representations of Change

The notion of change through time is central to the modeling techniques developed here, and the reader is familiarized with the use of *difference equations* to represent processes of change. Difference equation models rest upon well-developed mathematical theory,[1] enabling a straightforward and complete analysis of a process through time. They do not, however, require advanced mathematical training to be understood. A large majority of what follows requires only that readers possess a working knowledge of high school algebra and, perhaps, some patience.

Difference equation models are not the only dynamic models that can represent change in some phenomenon over time. Time can be treated as continuous, thereby producing differential equation models based on infinitely small time units and instantaneous rates of change. In difference equations time is treated as a series of discrete, equally spaced units. The choice between analogous pairs of difference and differential equation models is easily made when phenomena have a natural time metric in either discrete or continuous time. There are often grounds, however, for viewing discrete events as manifestations of an underlying continuous process, or continuous processes as being manifested at discrete points in time, and hence the argument that phenomena have a "natural" representation in discrete or continuous time is frequently undermined. Indeed, arguments can be made to justify representing most processes as either discrete or continuous (Kohfeld and Salert, 1982).

Several considerations lead us to develop dynamic models as discrete time representations. First, observations *always* occur in discrete time. In the physical sciences observations can be taken in such rapid succession that they approach a continuous observation, but this is seldom the case in the social sciences. Data on social phenomena are typically available at discrete time points that are significantly separated in time. For example, a scientist who is interested in the cooling process of a heated liquid takes thousands of measurements separated only by small fractions of a second. A social scientist who is interested in the socialization process of a young child acquires far fewer measurements that are much farther apart in time. As a result, we frequently base our representation on the observed behavior rather than the underlying process.

Second, given analogous difference and differential equations, difference equation models are capable of representing a wider variety of possible behavior patterns over time, and thus offer greater possibilities for modeling observed behaviors with simpler models. This feature of difference equations is convenient, but also mildly disturbing. It suggests that the choice of a modeling strategy and an accompanying representation for time is not merely a technical matter unrelated to substantive considerations. Rather, the choice of discrete time models rather than continuous time models has important substantive implications (see the Appendix for a more complete discussion of these matters).

Finally, and not insignificantly, difference equation models require a lower level of mathematical sophistication. We could not hope to cover the same ground in the available space for the same readers if our development proceeded in terms of differential equation models.

We embrace the notion that any model serves only as an abstract representation of a process. Even in representing time we are forced to employ an abstraction with inevitable limitations. The models employed here should not be judged on the extent to which they *replicate* a social process, but rather on the extent to which they help us *understand* a social process.

Synchronic versus Diachronic Change

Throughout this monograph we utilize the concept of the *structure* of a dynamic process. By this we mean the laws of change that define the time-dependence of a process. The first objective of dynamic modeling is to understand, substantively, the mechanisms that are generating change in some observable phenomenon, and then to translate this set of ideas about structure into a mathematical language that can be deductively investigated.

The techniques presented here are intended to equip the reader with a set of tools for representing dynamic structures and investigating how such structures behave. It must be emphasized, however, that these technologies are only applicable to *synchronic change*—to change produced by a fixed dynamic structure. The treatment of *diachronic change*—the process of moving from one structure into another—requires different methodologies and is not considered here.

In Chapter 2, for example, we present a model of mobilization. We hypothesize a very elementary dynamic structure by which mobilization levels change from one point in time to the next. We use a difference equation model to represent this structure, and to study its properties. The problem of how one mobilization process is transformed into another, however, cannot be addressed within this technology. Our modeling allows us to learn essentially all there is to know about any particular mobilization process; it may even help to understand the conditions that will cause one process to break down and be replaced by another. But it will not allow us to deduce what new structure will emerge. Theories attempting to explain the origin of a new dynamic structure, or the replacement of one structure by another, are beyond the bounds of the models considered here.[2]

Dynamic Models and Other Models of Change

Recent developments in social science research have more and more come to include time as an important explanatory concept. Dynamic modeling is only one means for addressing the importance of time and change, and it is valuable to juxtapose dynamic models with other models and approaches for understanding social processes and social change.

Various statistical strategies, and particularly statistical time series analysis, are frequently used to incorporate time within social science explanations. For example, Tufte (1978) uses a statistical strategy to relate economic conditions in the spring to election outcomes in the subsequent fall. Lewis-Beck and Alford (1980) use a time series design to relate policy interventions in coal mines with changes over time in mine safety. And, Hibbs (1976) uses a different time series design to show the over-time relationship between unemployment rates and labor union militance. Many of these efforts rest upon a well-developed econometrics literature that is concerned with a variety of estimation problems. Indeed, a continuing line of inquiry is related to many of the estimation issues that arise within time series designs (Ostrom, 1978).

Dynamic models are complementary to these statistical approaches, but they are distinct from them as well. This is not to say that issues in statistical estimation are irrelevant to dynamic models: One strategy for obtaining values for structural parameters within a dynamic model is to estimate them statistically. Indeed, during the course of our development we statistically estimate model parameters in several different instances. The important point remains: *Dynamic modeling is not a statistical technique*, and this monograph is not statistical in content.

The Structure of the Presentation

This monograph considers four general types of increasingly complex dynamic models in the ensuing four chapters. These chapters deal, respectively, with single-equation linear models, single-equation nonlinear models, linear systems composed of linear interdependent equations, and nonlinear systems composed of nonlinear interdependent equations. The substantive topics of these models—political mobilization, social diffusion, arms races, and competition over scarce resources—are fundamental to a variety of social science concerns but incidental to the objective of the manuscript. The substantive topics are used essentially as vehicles for introducing a series of issues related to dynamic modeling in discrete time, and these issues are germane to an even broader range of substantive concerns.

In summary, our goal is to present a framework for considering the logical consequences of a social process with a particular and specified structure. The reader who perseveres will acquire an overview of four broad classes of models and an understanding of the research situations in which they are substantively appropriate and likely to be useful. In addition, we hope that some specific modeling strategies will be acquired in the form of mathematical representations for frequently recurring social phenomena. We begin our task by developing a dynamic model of the political mobilization process.

2. FIRST-ORDER LINEAR DIFFERENCE EQUATION MODELS: A MODEL OF THE MOBILIZATION PROCESS

This chapter examines some elementary ideas regarding political mobilization and develops a dynamic model of the mobilization process. We begin with a set of statements about mobilization mechanisms. These statements are then translated into a formal, mathematical representation. Finally, techniques for analyzing and estimating the model are introduced. During the course of developing this model, we define and illustrate a number of ideas that are central to dynamic modeling. These include difference equations and their solutions, the equilibrium of a dynamic process, system stability, and qualitative behaviors over time. By introducing these concepts within the context of a particular model, the power of dynamic technologies as a strategy for investigating social and political problems becomes apparent.

Mobilization Processes

Social and political events occur at specific times and in specific contexts, but they are seldom divorced from the past or from the future. Many of these events are imbedded within processes that can be best understood as occurring across time. Political or social mobilization—the recruitment of individuals to some cause (or party or belief or practice)—is one such phenomenon. A current mobilization level is inherently dependent upon mobilization in the past, just as future mobilization is tied to mobilization in the present. In short, the process of mobilization is *time-dependent* in the sense of being sequenced. *Future levels* of mobilization are intimately connected with *past levels* according to a systematic dynamic structure. Using a dynamic model, then, we wish to develop a specific representation of the logic underlying *change* in mobilization levels from one point in time to the next.

A First Dynamic Model: The Gain/Loss Formulation

Any population can be usefully partitioned into two groups relative to the mobilization process: those individuals who are currently mobilized and those who are not. Denote as M_t the proportion of the relevant population which is mobilized at time t. Since the partitioning is exhaustive, the proportion of the population that is not mobilized at time t is given by the quantity $1 - M_t$. M_t is in principle observable, and it is formally known as a *system state*—a numeric quantity characterizing a process at a point in time.

The problem is to model the change in M_t across discrete points in time. Change in M_t may be written formally as:

$$\Delta M_t = M_{t+\tau} - M_t \qquad [2.1]$$

where τ is the *differencing interval*. For our treatment of discrete-time dynamics, the differencing interval is always assumed to be unity unless otherwise noted. While the assumption of $\tau = 1$ is a standard modeling practice, the essential point for technical development is that τ is fixed. A linear transformation can always be used to obtain a τ^* that has the value unity and similarly, the inverse transformation can be used to recover the interval in its original units. We also follow the usual practice of developing difference equation dynamics as functions on the integers, but the key formal properties are a *fixed difference interval* and a well-defined, uninterrupted *sequence*.

We thus define the first difference of M_t as:

$$\Delta M_t = M_{t+1} - M_t \qquad [2.2]$$

Higher-order differences obtained by continued differencing of the dynamic equation are considered in later chapters.

A change in the level of political mobilization, ΔM_t, results from two simultaneous sources. From time t to (t + 1) some individuals who are not mobilized will be recruited, generating a *gain* in M_t. Some other individuals who have already been mobilized will defect, thus producing a *loss* in M_t. The net effect of these simultaneous (but independent) gains and losses gives the change in M_t, ΔM_t.

Let a constant parameter, g, represent the probability that an un-mobilized individual is mobilized from time t to (t + 1). Then the gain in M_t is given by the recruitment rate, g, multiplied times the unmobilized population, $(1 - M_t)$:

$$\text{gain of recruits} = g(1 - M_t) \qquad [2.3]$$

Similarly, define a second constant parameter, f, to represent the probability that an individual who is mobilized at t will case to be mobilized at (t + 1). The loss in M_t is calculated as this defection rate multiplied times the mobilized population:

$$\text{loss of members} = fM_t \qquad [2.4]$$

Thus, change in mobilization across time is given by:

$$\Delta M_t = g(1 - M_t) - fM_t \qquad [2.5]$$

(Change = gains - losses)

Equation 2.5 is the simplest form of a large family of *gain/loss models* whose underlying logic expresses the change in some state of a system as the sum of gains and losses that have occurred.

The two parameters, g and f, can be interpreted either as *rates* or as *probabilities*. Given a rate interpretation, the parameters express the *proportions* of the member and nonmember population partitions that change their behavior from t to (t + 1). Alternatively, the parameters may be viewed as the *probabilities* that an average member of either group changes his or her behavior. This probabilistic interpretation does not, of course, change the deterministic nature of the model itself. Regardless of whether one thinks of g and f as rates or as probabilities, both parameters are logically restricted to the (0,1) interval.

Within these (0,1) bounds, the magnitudes of both g and f depend upon the time metric chosen to represent a process. This dependence is easily illustrated by comparing presidential popularity to peasant farmers' adoption of agricultural innovations. Investigators may focus on short-term fluctuations (τ of one month), or longer-term fluctuations (τ of one year). Months might be more appropriate for presidential popularity, and years might be more appropriate for changes in peasant agricultural practices.

The descriptive adequacy of equation 2.5 is considerably improved by the incorporation of one additional idea. For many mobilization processes, some individuals are simply not susceptible to recruitment efforts under any circumstances. Our model accommodates this notion by letting an additional parameter, W, represent the proportion of individuals in the population who cannot or will not be mobilized. We wish to remove those individuals from consideration, and so the term 1 - W gives the maximum mobilization level possible. At any particular moment, then, the population susceptible to recruitment is given by the quantity $1 - W - M_t$. It is convenient, however, to define the quantity.

$$L = 1 - W \qquad [2.6]$$

such that L may be interpreted as the upper limit on the potentially mobilized population. Substituting, our model becomes:

$$\Delta M_t = g(L - M_t) - fM_t \qquad [2.7]$$

The parameter W (or L) has a substantive and logical status somewhat different from that of g and f—the gain and loss rate parameters. The quantities g and f are rates or probabilities, while the parameter W (or L) is measured in the metric of the state M_t, and constitutes a modification in the description of the population that is subject to the mobilization process. In a purely formal sense, g, f, and W are all parameters of the process, but in a substantive sense, g and f have a different epistemological status when contrasted with W. Put another way, W describes while g and f give laws of change.

The model treats the population of interest as three distinct groups: the mobilized (M_t), the unmobilized subject to recruitment ($L - M_t$), and those who *cannot* be mobilized ($W = 1 - L$). The state variable M_t is observable and subject to variation across time. The parameters f, g, and L are assumed to be invariant over time; they are *not* directly observable and must be estimated empirically.

Throughout this chapter the gain/loss model is discussed in terms of political parties and their electoral support.This convention facilitates our discussion, but should not obscure the broad substantive applicability of the model. This particular model, and others similar to it, are useful in understanding a wide range of social and political phenomena: support for political candidates during a campaign, changes in consumer preference, adoption of birth control practices, disapproval of the Vietnam War, and so forth.

Difference Equations as Representations of Change

Equation 2.7 expresses the *logic* of the model most directly. In analyzing difference equation models, however, it is convenient to rearrange the original substantive specification algebraically in order to produce the following standard form:

$$M_{t+1} = a_0 + a_1 M_t \qquad [2.8]$$

This is readily accomplished by recalling that

$$\Delta M_t = M_{t+1} - M_t \qquad [2.9]$$

Substituting equation 2.9 into equation 2.7 and expanding yields

$$M_{t+1} - M_t = gL - gM_t - fM_t \qquad [2.10]$$

or, regrouping and collecting terms:

$$M_{t+1} = gL + (1 - f - g)M_t \qquad [2.11]$$

The reader should verify that equation 2.11 is in the standard form for first-order linear difference equations given by equation 2.8, with

$$a_0 = gL \qquad [2.12]$$

$$a_1 = 1 - f - g \qquad [2.13]$$

The standard form of equation 2.11 is crucial to an understanding of the mobilization model's mathematical and deductive properties. We characterize this form as a *first-order linear difference equation with constant coefficients*. The dynamics are expressed as a *difference equation*, because time is taken as a series of discrete, equally spaced events, and because system states are sequenced on time (i.e., they are time dependent). The equation is *linear*, because none of the a_i coefficients are a function of any of the states of the system (the M_{t-k} for $k = 0, 1, 2, \ldots$). Notice that the distinction between "nonlinear" and "linear" difference equations is unrelated to the shape of the generated time path for the system state. Linear models typically produce nonlinear paths, as do nonlinear models.

The equation has *constant coefficients* because the a_i are functions of fixed model parameters (g, f, L) that do not vary over time—a typical simplifying assumption. Finally, the *order* of a difference equation gives the maximum number of lags required to generate any particular observation in time; it is determined by subtracting the lowest time subscript in the equation from the highest time subscript. In this instance only one time point in the past is required to predict the next point, and hence the model is *first order*:

$$(t + 1) - t = 1 \qquad [2.14]$$

More complex difference equations are addressed in subsequent chapters. As we shall see, however, the first-order linear difference equation with constant coefficients is a powerful tool for analyzing and describing laws of change.

The next task is to ascertain the specific deductive consequences of the intuitive ideas regarding mobilization that are expressed in the model. What does the model assert, substantively, about mobilization processes? What histories of mobilization does it predict, under what circumstances? How well do these predictions stand against data? In order to address these issues, we briefly introduce the idea of *solutions* to difference equations and the techniques by which such solutions are derived.

Solutions to First-Order Difference Equations

A solution to a difference equation is a single function that generates a sequence of values satisfying the difference equation at each time point (Goldberg, 1958). The solution for equation 2.8 is developed in a straightforward fashion by first generating a series of equations that calculate several successive states as functions of the initial condition.

$$M_1 = a_0 + a_1 M_0$$

$$M_2 = a_0 + a_1 M_1 = a_0 + a_1 a_0 + a_1^2 M_0$$

$$M_3 = a_0 + a_1 M_2 = a_0 + a_1 a_0 + a_1^2 a_0 + a_1^3 M_0$$

$$M_n = a_0 + a_1 M_{n-1}$$

$$= a_0 + a_1 a_0 + a_1^2 a_0 + \ldots + a_1^{n-1} a_0 + a_1^n M_0$$

$$M_n = a_1^n M_0 + \sum_{i=1}^{n} a_1^{i-1} a_0 \qquad [2.15]$$

Suppose that $a_1 = 0$. Then what happens? Clearly

$$M_n = a_0 \qquad [2.16]$$

for all time. Thus, the process is stationary, and the future is constant.

Alternatively, suppose that $a_0 = 0$ and invoke equation 2.15 once again. In this instance the process *is* time dependent and defined as

$$M_n = a_1^n M_0 \qquad [2.17]$$

These two hypothesized conditions ($a_0 = 0$ and $a_1 = 0$) demonstrate that a generated sequence will fail to be dynamically interesting unless a_1 is different from zero. (Although, as we will see below, it is still possible for a_1 to be different from zero and for the generated sequence to be constant over time.)

Equation 2.15 fulfills the definition for a solution to a difference equation by generating a sequence that satisfies the difference equation at each time point, but it offers little advantage over the alternative method for calculating M_n—successive calculations using the original dynamic equation. More importantly, it is not *analytically* useful. The solution becomes more instructive when it is translated into its closed form.

Begin by expressing equation 2.15 as

$$M_n = S + a_1^n M_0 \qquad [2.18]$$

where

$$S = a_0 + a_1 a_0 + a_1^2 a_0 + \ldots + a_1^{n-1} a_0 \qquad [2.19]$$

Multiply both sides of equation 2.19 by a_1 to produce

$$a_1 S = a_1 a_0 + a_1^2 a_0 + \ldots + a_1^n a_0 \qquad [2.20]$$

Finally, subtract equation 2.20 from equation 2.19, and divide both sides by $1 - a_1$, given that $a_1 \neq 1$, to obtain

$$S = \frac{a_0(1 - a_1^n)}{1 - a_1} \qquad [2.21]$$

Substituting this formulation for S into equation 2.18 produces the following closed-form solution for the equation 2.8 difference equation:

$$M_n = \frac{a_0 - a_0 a_1^n}{1 - a_1} + a_1^n M_0 \qquad [2.22]$$

This solution is clearly degenerate when $a_1 = 1$, producing a denominator of zero in the first term on the right-hand side. In this special case ($a_1 = 1$) the following closed-form solution is readily derived:

$$M_n = a_0 + a_1 M_{n-1} = n a_0 + M_0 \qquad [2.23]$$

Summarizing our results, first-order linear difference equations with constant coefficients, written in the standard form (from equation 2.8):

$$M_n = a_0 + a_1 M_{n-1}$$

have solutions given by (from equations 2.22 and 2.23, respectively):

$$M_n = \frac{a_0 - a_0 a_1^n}{1 - a_1} + a_1^n M_0 \qquad \text{(for } a_1 \neq 1\text{)}$$

$$M_n = n a_0 + M_0 \qquad \text{(for } a = 1\text{)}$$

Furthermore, it can be shown (Goldberg, 1958) that *these are the only solutions*. Thus, given any dynamic model written in the form of a first-order linear difference equation with constant coefficients, we are able to obtain a solution; and once the parameters a_0 and a_1 are known, we can directly ascertain the value of the time series at any n^{th} point in time.

The utility of the solution goes far beyond merely calculating sequence values. We wish to interpret the solution substantively, and it is to this substantive potential that we now turn.

Equilibrium and Stability

Before treating equilibrium in its technical aspects, several substantive examples are in order. The general level of partisan support for a political party in the United States exhibits remarkable stability over long time periods, often referred to as political epochs (Burnham, 1970). These periods are typically ushered in by an election or series of elections in which a rapid change in relative party fortunes is registered. This well-known phenomenon in American electoral history is an example of a dynamic system that experiences a fundamental alteration: an important parameter or input changes, producing rapid adjustment of the process to a new *equilibrium*. Equilibrium does not mean the absence of change in individual behavior but rather the typical steadiness of a measure of behavior. That is to say, equilibrium as a technical concept refers to a numerical measure of the level of the process. Clearly there are an unlimited number of ways in which the Democratic party might receive 58% of the presidential vote from election to election. People die, new electors join, citizenship is granted to immigrants, general levels of partisanship may change, yet the percentage *may appear nearly constant*. It is likely that this is a substantive example of equilibrium. Indeed, as we show below, the Democratic revolution of the 1930s can be interpreted in this fashion by means of the first-order difference equation model.

An *equilibrium value* for a linear difference equation may be thought of as a steady state that is independent of time (May, 1974), and a difference equation sequence is in equilibrium if the sequence remains constant over time. The discrete-time system is said to be *stable* if the generated sequence returns toward equilibrium after a disturbance moves it away from equilibrium. Thus, in terms of political mobilization, a mobilization process is approximately at equilibrium when the support of a political party remains constant through successive elections.

The reader should understand that equilibrium does not imply stasis or a lack of dynamics—it does not require that all supporters stay supporters nor that all nonsupporters remain unrecruited. Indeed, so long as recruitment and defection rates differ from zero, defections and recruitment *must* occur, even at equilibrium. Rather, in equilibrium all motion is balanced such that defections are perfectly offset by new recruitment. Under equilibrium it is the *net* change that is zero, not all change in the system. In formal terms, the *number* describing successive states of the system does not change.

By convention, if a dynamic equation specifies some system state S_t, the equilibrium value for S_t is denoted as S^*. Note that the time subscript disappears, since the equilibrium value is not (by definition) time dependent. The equilibrium value for our mobilization model may be found in a number of ways. Perhaps the most intuitive is to recall that at equilibrium, net change (here, ΔM_t) is zero. If we then set the original dynamic equation to zero, and substitute M^* for M_t on the right-hand side, we may solve for M^* (from equation 2.7):

$$\Delta M_t = g(L - M_t) - fM_t$$

and at equilibrium

$$\Delta M_t = 0 \qquad \text{(by definition)}$$

so

$$0 = g(L - M^*) - fM^*$$

or

$$M^* = \frac{gL}{f + g} = \left(\frac{g}{f + g}\right)L \qquad [2.24]$$

And, if the first-order equation is written in standard form (from equation 2.8):

$$M_{t+1} = a_0 + a_1 M_t$$

it is easily shown that

$$M^* = a_0/(1 - a_1) = (gL)/(f + g) \quad \text{(see equations} \qquad [2.25]$$
$$\text{2.12 and 2.13)}$$

Equations 2.24 and 2.25 reveal an important feature of equilibrium. The equilibrium is independent of initial conditions: The process has an outcome that is divorced from its origins!

As equation 2.24 indicates, the equilibrium also has a direct interpretation in terms of model parameters. Recall that L is expressed in the same metric as M_t, whereas g and f are rates or probabilities. The equilibrium is the product of (1) the available population, L, and (2) the ratio of the recruitment rate, g, to the sum of the recruitment and defection rates, g + f. Thus, if L = 0 or if g = 0 the equilibrium will equal zero because no one is available to be recruited in the first instance, and because none of those available *are* recruited in the second instance. If f = 0, the equilibrium will equal L because continually occurring recruitments are never offset by defections! Thus, equation 2.24 emphasizes the differences in the substantive status of model parameters: g and f are the structural parameters underlying the process, whereas L is a description of the population—a population parameter.

The solution to the dynamic equation not only ascertains the exact path of a mobilization process; it also provides a basic understanding of stability and qualitative behavior over time. In first-order linear difference equations with constant coefficients, the parameter a_1 is crucial to this understanding. Depending upon the value of a_1, a sequence may be produced that is (1) unstable and diverges toward positive and (or) negative infinity either monotonically or with period two oscillation,[3] or (2) stable and converges toward an equilibrium point, M*, either monotonically or with period two oscillation, or (3) constant and maintains its initial condition through time. These are the only qualitative behaviors that are possible.

General criteria for these behaviors are obtained directly from the general solution for first-order linear difference equations with constant coefficients. Recall that this solution is given by:

$$M_n = \frac{a_0 - a_0 a_1^n}{1 - a_1} + a_1^n M_0 \qquad (\text{for } a_1 \neq 1) \qquad [2.26]$$

An inspection of this equation shows that the absolute value of the generated series will approach infinity whenever a_1 is greater than 1 or less than −1. Conversely, if a_1 lies within the (−1,+1) interval, then both of the a_1^n terms approach 0 in the limit. Thus, for successively larger values of n, the sequence approaches the limiting value,

$$a_0/(1 - a_1) = M^* \quad \text{(see equation 2.25)} \qquad [2.27]$$

A constant sequence is produced by a special set of circumstances. When a_1 does not equal 1, and when

$$M_0 = a_0/(1 - a_1) = M^* \qquad [2.28]$$

the resulting sequence begins in equilibrium and remains so.

What can be said regarding the behavior of the sequence as it converges toward equilibrium or diverges toward infinity? Returning to the solution for equation 2.22, notice that a_1^t oscillates between negative and positive values if a_1 is negative. Alternatively, a_1^t grows or decays monotonically (i.e., ever increasing or decreasing) whenever a_1 is positive. Thus, both stability (convergence or divergence with respect to equilibrium), and qualitative behavior (monotonic or oscillatory trajectories) depend exclusively on the magnitude of a_1, and are not affected by either the initial condition, M_0, or by a_0—the exogenous input to the process. These results concerning convergence, divergence, monotonicity, and oscillation are summarized and illustrated in Figure 2.1.

Substantive Applications

The mathematical properties of first-order linear difference equations with constant coefficients have important implications for our model of mobilization. We have derived the equilibrium mobilization level, M^*, and have given it direct substantive interpretation. But is the equilibrium point a stable one? What are the political conditions that produce an unstable or divergent mobilization process? A stable one?

Before answering these questions, we must review the descriptive constraints upon model parameters. Because each parameter represents a substantive concept that is tied to the logic of the model, each is subject to certain definitional contraints. As was discussed above, both the recruitment and defection parameters (g and f) must lie within the zero-one interval. Similarly, because the upper limit (L) is a proportion, it too must be bounded by the zero (no one) to unity (everyone) range.

Recall that the trajectory of M_t converges toward M^* if and only if the absolute value of a_1 is less than 1. That is, for our model to be stable (converge on M^*), we require that:

$$-1 < (1 - f - g) < 1 \quad \text{or} \quad -1 < a_1 < 1 \qquad [2.29]$$

Thus, given the descriptive constraint that

$$0 < f, g, L < +1 \qquad [2.30]$$

inequality 2.29 must always be true. The mobilization model describes a process that is inherently stable, as it must be. If our model predicted that mobilization would grow or decay to positive or negative infinity over time, we would clearly have to rethink our specification!

But will convergence toward equilibrium be a smooth, monotonic approach or a more erratic oscillatory one? It was demonstrated that whenever a_1 is negative, the time path of the difference equation will oscillate with period two, but when a_1 is positive the time path will be monotonic. In terms of the model, then, if

$$(1 - f - g) < 0 \qquad [2.31]$$

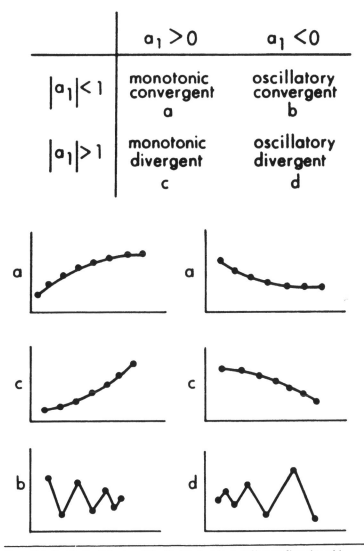

Figure 2.1 Qualitative Behavior of the First-Order Linear Difference Equation with Constant Coefficients ($M_0 \neq M^*$)

mobilization will exhibit an "erratic" oscillatory convergence toward M^*, but if the inequality is reversed, the time-path will monotonically grow (if $M_0 < M^*$) or decay (if $M_0 > M^*$) toward equilibrium. Put another way, if $(1 - f) > g$, then convergence is monotonic, but if $(1 - f) < g$, then convergence is oscillatory.

What interpretation may be given to the quantity $1 - f$? Recall that f is the defection rate, or the probability that a mobilized individual ceases to be mobilized. The quantity $1 - f$, then, gives the probability that a mobilized individual remains mobilized; that is, $1 - f$ is the *retention rate* for the mobilization process. Thus, whenever the retention rate exceeds the recruitment rate, the mobilization process is monotonic toward M^*—the process moves smoothly. But if the recruitment rate exceeds the rate of retention, the process continually overdrives the equilibrium point, and convergence is oscillatory. Simply, if a party recruits individuals faster than it retains them, the mobilization process is an erratic, oscillatory one. This is an intuitively satisfying result: Given our knowledge regarding human behavior and the stability of partisan attachments, $1 - f$ is not likely to be less than g except in times of extreme political upheaval. These results are illustrated in Figure 2.2.

Model Estimation

The use of discrete-time dynamic models is not limited to the mathematical simulation of social and political phenomena; they can be used to analyze empirically observed processes as well. In this section model estimation is demonstrated through a consideration of Democratic mobilization in Lake County, Indiana, from 1920 through 1968. This period is an important one in Democratic party politics including the return to normalcy following World War I, the Great Depression and the New Deal, the Eisenhower era, Vietnam, and the political turbulence of the 1960s. Lake County, which includes the city of Gary, is appropriate to our investigation because it has historically contained large concentrations of the population groups upon which Democratic ascendancy has been based: industrial workers, blacks, and the poor.

Whenever a dynamic model is written in linear form, it can, at least in principle, be estimated by ordinary least squares (OLS). Estimates are readily obtained for the coefficients on the states of the dynamic equation, but some knotty statistical problems result whenever a regression equation includes lagged endogenous variables—prior values of dependent variables that are treated as independent variables (Schrodt and Ward, 1981; Ostrom, 1978). This problem is an important one for dynamic modeling because statements of change explain the present in terms of the past. A number of solutions to these problems have been suggested (Hibbs, 1974), and we make no attempt to expand on them here. The goal of the present section is only to demonstrate one model estimation strategy; the statistical estimates themselves should be evaluated with appropriate suspicion.

The model written in standard form (from equation 2.11):

$$M_{t+1} = gL + (1 - f - g)M_t$$

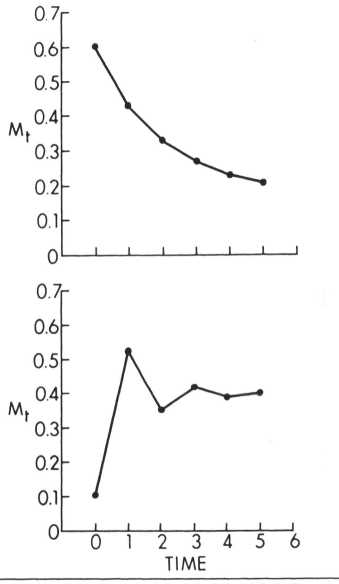

Figure 2.2 Monotonic Convergence: (g = .1, f = .3, L = .7, M_0 = .6, 1 − f = .7)
Oscillatory Convergence: (g = .7, f = .7, L = .8, M_0 = .1, 1 − f = .3)

is isomorphic to the OLS statistical model

$$Y = m_0 + m_1 X_1 \quad (+ \text{ error}) \tag{2.32}$$

where m_1 is the slope and m_0 the intercept of the statistical model. The dynamic model is estimated by OLS, with the following mappings:

$Y = M_{t+1}$ = the proportion of Lake County adults voting for the Democratic candidate in year $t + 1$, for $t + 1 = 1924$, $1928, \ldots, 1968$

$X_1 = M_t$ = the lag of Y, i.e., the proportion of adults voting Democratic in year t, for $t = 1920, 1924, \ldots, 1964$

$$\hat{m}_0 = gL = \quad 0.14 \quad \text{(by OLS)} \tag{2.33}$$

$$\hat{m}_1 = (1 - f - g) = 0.62 \quad \text{(by OLS)} \tag{2.34}$$

We have readily obtained estimates for the slope and intercept, m_0 and m_1, but it is more difficult to obtain parameter estimates for f, g, and L from these statistical estimators. For many models this is a simple task, with the statistical estimators mapping directly to the model parameters. Unfortunately, that is not the case here: We must solve for three unknowns (f, g, L) from only two mapping equations. Because we have fewer equations than unknowns (i.e., insufficient information), the mapping structure is *underdetermined* and cannot be solved without additional information.

It is worth noting that even if no additional restriction can be imposed to determine the parameters uniquely, the equilibrium value, M^*, may be directly obtained from the empirically estimated coefficients ($\hat{m}_0$ and $\hat{m}_1$) because (from equation 2.26):

$$M^* = a_0/(1 - a_1)$$

or, in current notation,

$$\hat{M}^* = \hat{m}_0/(1 - \hat{m}_1) = 0.14/(1 - 0.62) = .37$$

Because m_0 and m_1 are known from estimation, M^* is uniquely determined! Thus, in spite of our lack of knowledge of parameter values, we have still determined that the Democratic mobilization equilibrium for Lake County is approximately 37% of the adult population.

The simplest solution to the problem of model underdetermination is to set L equal to 1. That is, assume that everyone in the Lake County adult population is a potential recruit to the Democratic party. This assumption produces a system of two equations and two unknowns and is *exactly determined* (and solvable) as follows:

$$g = m_0 \tag{2.35}$$

$$f = 1 - m_0 - m_1 \qquad [2.36]$$

While this procedure does provide rough estimates of f and g, it is less than satisfactory: We know that L is almost certainly less than 1, not only for Democratic mobilization in Lake County, but for most interesting social processes in most environments.

Fortunately, it is possible to utilize prior knowledge about the model and its parameters to derive unique estimates for all three unknowns. Based upon our requirement that all three model parameters must lie in the (0,1) interval, and upon inequalities 2.33 and 2.34, we first establish that:

$$0 < m_0/g < 1 \qquad [2.37]$$

This inequality holds because L equals m_0/g *and* it lies in the (0,1) interval. Further, because g is always positive,

$$0 < m_0 < g \qquad [2.38]$$

As a second step we rearrange inequality 2.34 to produce

$$f = 1 - g - m_1 \qquad [2.39]$$

And, because f also lies in the unit interval

$$0 < 1 - g - m_1 < 1 \quad \text{or} \quad -m_1 < g < 1 - m_1 \qquad [2.40]$$

Thus, from inequalities 2.38 and 2.40 we know that an *upper bound* for g is $1 - m_1$ and a *lower bound* is m_0.

Collecting our results, g lies in an interval bounded by m_0 and $1 - m_1$. Lacking better information it is reasonable to estimate that g lies at the midpoint of the $(m_0, 1 - m_1)$ interval. If we assume that a normal distribution of estimates lies within this interval, then the likelihood of choosing an accurate estimate for g is maximized at the midpoint. Treating our parameter estimates in such a manner is entirely reasonable because our choice of time points and elections is only a sampling from a universe of mobilization estimates: off-year elections, state-level elections, and so forth.

Assuming that g lies at the midpoint of the $(m_0, 1 - m_1)$ interval produces a third equation that exactly determines the system mappings. We obtain as an estimate of g the midpoint given by:

$$g = m_0 + (1 - m_1 - m_0)/2 = (1 + m_0 - m_1)/2 \qquad [2.41]$$

The reader should verify that our remaining mappings, when this estimate of g is utilized, become:

$$f = 1 - m_1 - g = (1 - m_0 - m_1)/2 \qquad [2.42]$$

$$L = m_0/g = 2m_0/(1 + m_0 - m_1) \qquad\qquad [2.43]$$

Using this additional constraint, the OLS estimates of m_0 and m_1 produce a set of parameter estimates for Lake County that are quite plausible: $g = 0.26$, $f = 0.12$, and $L = 0.54$. Thus, the estimated Democratic recruitment rate during the period was twice the estimated defection rate, but nearly half of the eligible population was not susceptible to Democratic mobilization.[4]

Figure 2.3 displays three mobilization time series for Lake County: (1) the observed sequence, (2) the completely deterministic time path generated by the estimated parameters with the observed 1920 mobilization level as the initial condition, and (3) the time path generated by the estimated parameters using each observed mobilization level, M_t, to generate a predicted level, $\hat{M}_{t+1}$. The estimated mobilization model generates a monotonically increasing sequence that converges on an equilibrium value ($\hat{M}^*$) of 0.37. Notice, however, that the observed mobilization levels shown in Part A of Figure 2.3 tend to bounce around the predicted time path shown in Part B of the same figure—a deterministic time path that is generated using the previously estimated parameters with the observed 1920 mobilization level as an initial condition. This is fully expected because we have attempted to model only the most basic mobilization mechanism without regard to short-term exogenous factors. The predicted time path may be thought of as an idealized path toward equilibrium under the condition that no short-run forces operate after 1920. By contrast, the long-term behavior of the process *including* short-run forces, but still with convergence toward equilibrium, is graphed in Part C of Figure 2.3. That picture illustrates motion toward equilibrium that includes the first period recoveries from successive short-term perturbations. Because the estimates for model parameters are based upon the entire set of initial conditions, i.e., each observed point rather than just 1920, Part C presents the theoretically predicted time path arising from the estimated model.

These distinctions sometimes cause difficulties when first encountered. To fix ideas, keep in mind that one and only one equilibrium value is determined for a specified set of parameter values. On the other hand, *any* given value for M_t may be considered an (arbitrary) initial condition. The model specifies the laws of behavior for mobilization *in the short run*, but the general theory of linear difference equations discloses that the short-run law has a long-run consequence, namely, the limiting or equilibrium value toward which the process has a tendency to move after *any* displacement.

Recall equations 2.22 and 2.25, which give expressions for the closed-form solution and the equilibrium. These may be rewritten in a form that emphasizes the role of initial conditions as displacements from equilibrium

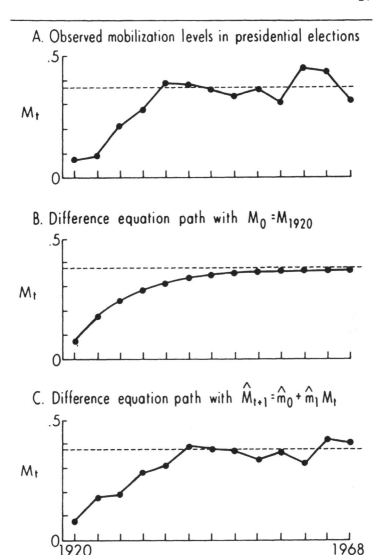

A. Observed mobilization levels in presidential elections

B. Difference equation path with $M_0 = M_{1920}$

C. Difference equation path with $\hat{M}_{t+1} = \hat{m}_0 + \hat{m}_1 M_t$

PRESIDENTIAL ELECTION YEAR

Figure 2.3 Democratic Mobilization in Lake County (1920-1968)

in determining the dynamics of the system. Equation 2.22 expressed the solution as

$$M_n = \frac{a_0 - a_0 a_1^n}{1 - a_1} + a_1^n M_0 \qquad (\text{for } a_1 \neq 1)$$

but rearrangement yields

$$M_n = \frac{a_0}{1 - a_1}(1 - a_1^n) + a_1^n M_0 \qquad [2.44]$$

And, on the basis of equation 2.25, we substitute to obtain

$$M_n = M^* (1 - a_1^n) + a_1^n M_0$$

$$M_n = \qquad M^* \qquad + a_1^n (M_0 - M^*)$$

$$M_n = \text{equilibrium} + (\text{decay})(\text{initial displacement}) \qquad [2.45]$$

Notice that the right-hand side of equation 2.45 can be read as decomposing some value of the process, say the nth, into an additive (linear) combination of the equilibrium, plus a contribution due to the initial displacement from equilibrium measured by the quantity $(M_0 - M^*)$, which in turn is weighted by the nth power of the parameter a_1. But exogenous, short-run disturbances do not allow the process to approach equilibrium asymptotically from a single initial condition. Rather, a whole series of new M_0's are introduced, and as the effect of an "old" M_0 fades away (as n grows large and a_1^n grows small), new initial conditions are constantly being introduced.

Reviewing, then, the interpretation of Figures 2.5 A-C is as follows. Figure 2.3A displays the data. Figure 2.3B displays the long-run path of recovery toward equilibrium associated with *only* the 1920 initial condition. Figure 2.3C displays the behavior of the process for multiple initial conditions, i.e., multiple exogenous short-run forces.

Summary

This chapter has introduced a number of concepts related to discrete time models of social and political processes. Our first mobilization model is quite elementary in its assumptions, and intentionally limited in its scope. Indeed, parts of the model are overly simplistic: Recruitment and defection rates are seldom constant over time; the direct dependence of current system states upon past states may extend farther back in time than just one time period; individual behavior is undoubtedly interdependent; and the world almost certainly is not linear for all processes and all times.

Nevertheless, the model serves to formalize a very basic social process, and increasingly complex models may be developed from this elementary building block. Increasing the complexity of a model does not guarantee that we will increase substantive understanding, however. Intentionally reduced systems models are often more insightful than their more "realistic" and hence more complex versions. If the modeler is sensitive to the assumptions they embody, first-order linear difference equations with constant coefficients can be powerful tools for the analysis of social and political change. With this caveat in mind, Chapter 3 once again addresses the topic of mobilization, but attempts to achieve greater realism by developing a nonlinear model of the mobilization process that incorporates the notion of social diffusion.

3. FIRST-ORDER NONLINEAR DIFFERENCE EQUATIONS: PROCESSES OF SOCIAL DIFFUSION

The social diffusion model developed in this chapter introduces a more sophisticated representation of change: the *nonlinear* first-order difference equation with constant coefficients. While the model is not especially complex either substantively or mathematically, it produces remarkably rich patterns of behavior over time. The model underscores the differences between nonlinear and linear dynamic processes. Solutions to nonlinear difference equations are rarely known, and no general technique exists for their discovery. The recursive form of this model, however, has been carefully analyzed, and it is possible to deduce its equilibria and qualitative behavior over time. (Recursive forms and other difference equation forms are defined in the Appendix.)

Models of this form have been used to explore such diverse applications as political mobilization, the adoption of birth control practices, and the spread of policy innovations. Typical applications include: (1) population demography, (2) social contagion and the spread of contagious diseases, (3) rumor spread, and (4) rapid changes in public opinion.

Mobilization Through Social Interaction

In Chapter 2 mobilization was modeled as a series of gains and losses at fixed rates. The *source* of change or system input, then, is constant through time. This constant source might be, for example, exposure to the media (if M_t represents support of the Vietnam War) or exposure to air pollution (if M_t represents lung cancer). But the critical assumption is that change is the result of constant source effects acting on individuals who are behaving independently of all other individuals in the population.

There are many instances when this assumption is untenable: The underlying dynamic structure results from the interaction of individuals, not from independent responses to constant source effects. That is, *individuals are exposed to other individuals*, and this interaction generates change over time. When this is the case, the logical form of the dynamic model becomes:

change = constant source gains — constant source losses + interaction gains (or losses)

Dynamic mechanisms that incorporate interaction effects have been demonstrated in a wide range of substantive applications. These include suicide rates (Durkheim, 1897), voting, turnout, and partisanship (Gosnell, 1927; Huckfeldt, 1979, 1980). Social interaction processes have also been demonstrated in such areas of behavior as choice of occupation, patient behavior in hospital wards, and racial attitudes. Dynamic treatments of social interaction processes have been provided by Przeworski and Sprague (1978), Coleman (1964), and McPhee (1963).

A Diffusion Model

In this section we develop a simple model of diffusion. Diffusion in human populations includes two central mechanisms: (1) a constant source of "exposure" and (2) spread from "interaction." Models of this kind can be interpreted either as probabilistic/stochastic or as deterministic. A model similar to the deterministic one developed here, but thoroughly stochastic, is known in the literature as a "pure birth process" model (Bartholomew, 1967). We are modeling *change* with a *mobilization* interpretation. But the interpretation might be disease, political information, product knowledge, rumor, or any other process characterized as diffusion or contagion. All have been studied using such models.

Suppose, then, that change in mobilization is composed of gains and losses. Furthermore, suppose that gains are obtained both from a constant source and from "social" interaction. Finally, assume that losses are not interactive but can be characterized as "spontaneous recovery." (For example, disease is self-limiting, "old" rumors are no longer of interest and hence forgotten, or memory erodes from simple time decay of information.) Thus, write

$$\Delta M_t = \text{source gains} + \text{interaction gains} - \text{decay losses} \qquad [3.1]$$

We partition the population, initially, into (1) those who have the disease, or know the information, or have heard the rumor, and (2) those who have not been exposed to the disease, or have not heard the rumor, or failed to learn the information. Thus, M_t is a *measure* in a *population* of *those possessing the property of interest.* Let M_t be measured by *counting* and express it as a proportion:

$$M_t = \frac{(\text{number of individuals with the property})}{(\text{total number of individuals in population})}$$

Similarly, those without the property may be measured as $(1 - M_t)$. Losses are treated as they were in the mobilization model in Chapter 2, but they could be elaborated in various ways. For now they are simply represented as $-fM_t$, where f represents the probability of members who no longer have the property leaving the group. In terms of our model then we have

$$\Delta M_t = \text{source gains} + \text{interaction gains} - fM_t \qquad [3.2]$$

Next we deal with gains. Define a quantity, L, in the metric of M_t as the upper limit of susceptibles. For example, there are always some in the population who are immune and will not catch a particular disease, some who are not in any communication network and will not hear the rumor, and some who will never form an unfavorable attitude about the president.

When Truman was at his lowest point of popularity, and when Nixon's popularity reached its lowest point after Watergate, the polls still showed that approximately 25% of the population still approved of both presidents. Thus, L is to be thought of as an upper bound, or natural limit on the "spread" of M_t. In this example, we think of M_t as (1) starting low (that is, $M_{t=0}$ approaches 0) and (2) growing in such a way that L is not exceeded. This second interpretative assumption furnishes a *constraint* on the parameters included in the model. Pictorially, the time path we have described is that displayed in Figure 3.1. Furthermore, we focus on "epochs" for diffusion during which conditions do not greatly change. Thus, we *fix parameters* as characteristic of a *time interval* of substantive interest, e.g., the length of an epidemic, the duration of a political campaign, or the time lapse between new and different scandals.

With these interpretations, then, L defines the whole population less nonsusceptibles, L = 1 − W. And, potential possessors may be written as

$$L - M_t$$

where

$$M_t < L \quad \text{always}$$

So we write, assuming fixed gains at rate g,

$$\Delta M_t = g(L - M_t) + \text{interaction gains} - fM_t \qquad [3.3]$$

Possible interpretations of $g(L - M_t)$ as gains from a constant source are that they could come from (1) radio broadcasts, (2) political pamphlets,

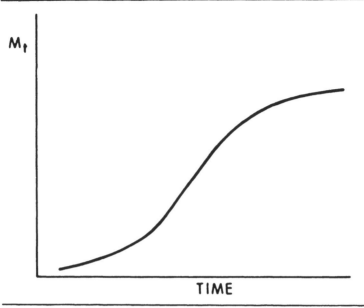

Figure 3.1 Time Path for a Diffusion Process

(3) newspapers, or (4) a contaminated well. Some readers may have noted that equation 3.3 includes a potential problem of double counting those who are recruited. We deal with this subsequently.

The theoretical problem, then, is that of abstractly characterizing an interaction mechanism in a convenient mathematical representation. We focus on the simplest possible social interaction, the minimal pair. Actually, most communication or social interaction is pairwise. Thus, considering interactions as only pairwise is not a serious simplification of social reality. The descriptive representation that we develop and offer as a model, however, is necessarily a simplification of the mechanisms through which pairwise interaction takes place.

· Let the pair (I,J) denote some form of interaction between I and J— a conversation, an observation, or any other form of social interaction. Let I_0 denote the fact that individual I does not have the property of interest, and let I_1 denote the fact that individual I does have that property. Similarly, let the absence or presence of the property in individual J be denoted as J_0 and J_1, respectively. Then there are four possible pairwise interactions between I and J: (I_0,J_0), (I_0,J_1), (I_1,J_0), and (I_1,J_1), such that, for example, (I_1,J_1) denotes the interaction of two mobilized individuals. In matrix form:

	Individual J	
	J_0	J_1
Individual I I_0	(I_0, J_0)	(I_0, J_1)
I_1	(I_1, J_0)	(I_1, J_1)

This construction underlies the assumption we make about mixing in the population, an assumption that is almost certainly oversimplified, but which is quite useful as a first approximation in representing diffusion phenomena. We assume, specifically, that each *interaction is pairwise and occurs randomly and independently among individuals in the population.* Thus, the probability that any interaction has components of a particular type is proportional to the frequency of the types in the population, i.e., proportional to the frequency of "0" and "1" type individuals.

In our case, one is or is not a member, one knows or does not know the information, one has or does not have the disease, and so forth. Clearly, the probability of an individual chosen at random at time t having the property of interest is given by M_t. The probability of not having the property is $1 - M_t$. But we are interested only in those interactions among persons who have the property and those who might acquire it through interaction. The expectation for those susceptible individuals in the population is, again, $L - M_t$. Assuming, then, that each interaction is random and independent, the probability of the pairwise interaction (I, J) being of a particular type is given by:

	J	
	J_0 $E(J_0) = L - M_t$	J_1 $E(J_1) = M_t$
I I_0 $E(I_0) = L - M_t$	$E(I_0, J_0) = (L - M_t)(L - M_t)$	$E(I_0, J_1) = M_t(L - M_t)$
I_1 $E(I_1) = M_t$	$E(I_1, J_0) = M_t(L - M_t)$	$E(I_1, J_1) = (M_t, M_t)$

The construction given above supplies our basic interactive rule.

Interactions of (M_t, M_t): no spread,
Interactions of $[(L - M_t), (L - M_t)]$: no spread,
Interactions of $[M_t, (L - M_t)]$: yield spread possibility, and
Interactions of $[(L - M_t), M_t]$: yield spread possibility.

From the matrix above it is evident that the relative frequency of pairwise interactions in the population between a mobilized individual and a potential recruit is given by: $2(L - M_t)M_t$. It is more convenient, however, to drop the doubling of the $(L - M_t)M_t$ quantity, and force the correction onto the parameter that gives the rate at which these "across group" interactions cause movement into or out of M_t. We denote this rate as the parameter s, and write:

$$\Delta M_t = g(L - M_t) + sM_t(L - M_t) - fM_t \qquad [3.4]$$

It would appear that we are finished. Notice, however, that the form of equation 3.4 might result in an individual being mobilized both from constant source effects and from interaction effects. Since an individual can become an M_t only once from time t to t + 1, we must correct for the potential double counting of gains from both constant source and interaction mechanisms.

The simplest repair for double counting is to make a time precedence assumption. The double counting may be corrected as follows: From the population being *exposed* to potential recruitment through social interaction, $(L - M_t)$, remove those *already recruited from constant source effects in an instant of time*. Hence, write

$$[(L - M_t) - g(L - M_t)] \qquad [3.5]$$

as the pool available for social interaction.

Our final elaboration of the diffusion model may be written, then, as:

$$\Delta M_t = g(L - M_t) + sM_t[(L - M_t) - g(L - M_t)] - fM_t \qquad [3.6]$$

where g and f give the gain and loss rates, respectively, in M_t resulting from constant source effects, and s gives the gain (or loss) in M_t from social interaction. Notice that while g and f have strict probabilistic interpretations, s is not sign restricted and is best interpreted as a rate parameter. Clearly, social interaction may result in new recruits (positive s) but also, perhaps, in loss of old members (negative s). Thus, there is no sign restriction on s.

Slightly more complex versions of the model are possible if we elaborate the loss term $-fM_t$, but we shall continue our analysis by considering only the most elementary case (from equation 3.6):

$$\Delta M_t = g(L - M_t) + sM_t[(L - M_t) - g(L - M_t)] - fM_t$$

Algebraic manipulation yields a quadratic form for the model:

$$\Delta M_t = (sg - s)M_t^2 + (sL - f - g - sgL)M_t + gL \qquad [3.7]$$

or by disaggregating the ΔM_t into $M_{t+1} - M_t$, obtain

$$M_{t+1} = (sg - s)M_t^2 + (1 + sL - f - g - sgL)M_t + gL \qquad [3.8]$$

The reader should verify that equation 3.8 is a first-order difference equation with constant coefficients. Note, however, that the dynamic equation is nonlinear, since one of the system states is squared (i.e., second-degree). The model, then, is a first-order quadratic difference equation with constant coefficients.

Parameter Restrictions

Descriptive adequacy imposes at least the following restriction:

$$0 \leqslant g,f \leqslant 1 \qquad [3.9]$$

but stronger restrictions for g and s may be required. From the model, the total gains evidently must satisfy the following inequality:

$$0 \leqslant g(L - M_t) + sM_t[(L - M_t) - g(L - M_t)] \leqslant (L - M_t) \qquad [3.10]$$

for: $0 \leqslant M_t \leqslant L$ and

$0 \leqslant g \leqslant 1$

And by imposing positive s: $0 < s$ $\qquad [3.11]$

Inequality 3.10 simply states that the total gains (change) must be positive or zero and less than or equal to the entire pool of susceptibles. Simplifying Inequality 3.10 we have

$$0 \leqslant g + sM_t(1 - g) \leqslant 1 \qquad M_t \neq L \qquad [3.12]$$

which may be written

$$0 \leqslant g(1 - sM_t) \leqslant (1 - sM_t) \qquad \text{yielding} \qquad [3.13]$$

$$0 \leqslant g \leqslant 1 \qquad [3.14]$$

which is exactly the same restriction assumed earlier. Similarly, we can solve inequality 3.10 for the restriction on s. Thus, we have

$$0 \leqslant g/(1 - g) + sM_t \leqslant 1/(1 - g) \qquad \text{for g not equal to 1} \qquad [3.15]$$

which reduces to

$$0 \leqslant s \leqslant 1/M_t \qquad \text{with } M_t > 0 \text{ and } s > 0 \qquad [3.16]$$

If $s < 0$, then inequalities 3.11 and 3.16 need no longer hold because the result of social interaction is to remove members from the population who have the property of interest, and the interaction term is a loss term. The reader might wish to develop the analogous parameter restrictions for the case $s < 0$.

Model Estimation

This model turns out to be nonlinear in its parameters (f, g, L, and s), but estimates for the parameters can be obtained if we impose an a priori hypothesis about L. The easiest solution to the problem is to set L equal to 1. That is, make the entire population susceptible for recruitment. If we set L at a particular value, the model is still nonlinear in parameters but now, unique estimates can be found. If we disaggregate ΔM_t and use algebraic manipulation, we can put the model in equation 3.7 into the following form:

$$M_{t+1} = (sg - s)M_t^2 + (1 + sL - f - g - sgL)M_t + gL \qquad [3.17]$$

This is equivalent to the least squares estimating form

$$Y = m_2X_2 + m_1X_1 + m_0 \quad (+ \text{ error}) \qquad [3.18]$$

where:

$$Y = M_{t+1}$$

$$X_2 = M_t^2$$

$$X_1 = M_t$$

It is instructive to note that the only set of observations required for estimation of this model is a time series of one state variable plus its lag. Using a time series of a single political variable, for example, we can investigate the relative contributions from constant sources (g and f) and from social interaction effects (s) with the same model. Least squares procedures may be used to obtain estimates of the coefficients m_i in equation 3.18. The estimating relationships for the parameters are specified by the system

$$sg - s \qquad\qquad = m_2 \qquad\qquad\qquad [3.19]$$

$$1 + sL - f - g - sgL = m_1$$

$$gL \qquad\qquad\qquad = m_0$$

For the simplest case assume that the entire population is susceptible, then $L = 1$. With this assumption system, equation 3.19 can be solved uniquely for the parameters s, g, and f in terms of the coefficient m_i as set forth below

$$f = 1 - m_0 - m_2 - m_1 \qquad\qquad\qquad [3.20]$$

$$g = m_0$$

$$s = m_2/(m_0 - 1)$$

Even though it is relatively easy to obtain values for the parameters using least squares estimation procedures, an explicit solution for the quadratic form of the first-order difference equation is not available. Conditions for convergence or divergence are known, however, as are tests that determine the qualitative nature of the time path. Furthermore, if the process is convergent, an explicit expression for the limit is available.

An Empirical Example

For illustrative purposes we have estimated the model using a time series of voting data for Essex County, Massachusetts. The time period examined is 1920 to 1972, and the vote used is Democratic vote for president, with M_t defined as the Democratic proportion of the presidential vote. (Data were collected from *America At The Polls* and *America Votes*, edited by Richard Scammon.) This covers the same period of Democratic mobilization as that used in Chapter 2, but uses a northeastern Democratic suburb of Boston.

Essex County parameter estimates, calculated from least squares coefficients using equation 3.20, are presented below.

Least squares coefficients:

$$\hat{m}_0 = 0.16 \quad \hat{m}_1 = 0.95 \quad \hat{m}_2 = -0.45 \qquad\qquad [3.21]$$

Parameter estimates:

when L = 1,   then   f = 0.34   g = 0.16   and   s = 0.54

when L = .74,   then   f = 0.25   g = 0.22   and   s = 0.57   [3.22]

Two sets of estimates were calculated from the m_t by setting L equal to 1 and .74, respectively. The value .74 for L might be justified by noting the residual support for Truman and Nixon at their lowest was about 25%. Furthermore, 74% is the highest Democratic proportion of the vote in Essex County during this period. Thus, it is perhaps reasonable to suppose about one-fourth of the voting population will *never* move to *any* cause—in Essex County, they will never become Democrats. The parameter values produced when L is set equal to one indicate that social interaction effects are stronger than individual level effects. (Essex County has a strong Democratic organization, which suggests that gains by the Democratic party are a result of interactions between Democratic supporters and recruitable nonsupporters.) The individual-level effects are also important, suggesting that national-level forces—social, economic, and political—are having an impact on individual voters in the county. Thus, national-level activity is inducing individual level *change* at the local level. Notice the change in the parameter estimates when L is set to .74. Social interaction effects are increased slightly, but individual loss effects are reduced. This provides support for earlier studies (Berelson et al., 1954; McPhee and Glaser, 1962) that indicated the importance of personal contact in mobilizing supporters.

Although we restricted the parameters f, g, and s, the values of the m_t were empirically determined *without* being subjected to any restrictions. One test of whether the model provides a reasonable explanation is to inspect the parameter estimates. If the estimated parameters meet the theoretically imposed, a priori restrictions (as they do in this instance), then this is additional evidence for the appropriateness of the model for analyzing the mobilization process. Again, the estimates were obtained using OLS, and these estimates should be evaluated using appropriate statistical caution due to the presence of lagged endogenous variables (see Hibbs, 1974).

Analyzing the Model

It should be emphasized at the outset that there are fundamental differences in the behavior of linear and nonlinear dynamics. For linear forms, theory is complete: A general solution can easily be found using the techniques presented in Chapters 2 and 4. The qualitative behavior of the system over time can also be deduced. Unfortunately, there is no standard technique for obtaining general solutions for nonlinear dynamic systems. Indeed, solutions to such systems are rarely known.

The problem is compounded by the fact that, unlike the linear dynamic system considered in the first chapter, nonlinear systems frequently exhibit multiple equilibria rather than a single, globally stable equilibrium point. Furthermore, the best general strategy is to ascertain the dynamic stability of some "neighborhood," or local region, around the equilibrium points. Only if the dynamic equations are linear will neighborhood stability and global stability necessarily be identical. This means that, whereas initial conditions do not affect long-run qualitative behavior in linear dynamic systems, *they can critically alter long-run behavior in nonlinear dynamic systems.*

Another complication that may arise from nonlinearity in the dynamic equations is that equilibrium need not be a point, but can be a *stable limit cycle.* As the term suggests, in a limit cycle the states of the system undergo cyclical patterns of change across time, and a stable limit cycle will return to its oscillatory trajectory after local perturbations (for more detailed technical discussion of these nonlinear system characteristics, see Rosen, 1970; Hirsch and Smale, 1974; and May, 1974).

Equilibrium Analysis

If a process is at point equilibrium, net change in its states is zero over time. Thus, at equilibrium, all successive values of M_t will be the same. That is, for a dynamic equation of order k, at equilibrium

$$M_{t+k} = M_t = M* \qquad [3.23]$$

where $M*$ is an equilibrium point (also termed a *stationary point*). We can then determine all values that satisfy equation 3.23 by setting ΔM_t equal to 0, substituting $M*$ for all M_t in the dynamic equation, and then solving for $M*$. Utilizing this procedure for our model gives

$$0 = (sg - s)M*^2 + (sL - f - g - sgL)M* + gL \qquad [3.24]$$

Equation 3.24 is simply a quadratic equation in $M*$, which may be solved by the quadratic formula. Recall that for an equation

$$0 = aX^2 + bX + c \qquad [3.25]$$

the solution for X is given by

$$X = (-b \pm \sqrt{b^2 - 4ac})/2a \qquad [3.26]$$

Equation 3.24 maps directly to 3.26, with

$$a = sg - s \qquad [3.27]$$

$$b = sL - f - g - sgL \qquad\qquad [3.28]$$

$$c = gL \qquad\qquad [3.29]$$

Thus solutions for equation 3.24 are given by the rather complex equation:

$$M^* = [-(sL - f - g - sgL)$$
$$\pm \sqrt{(sL - f - g - sgL)^2 - 4(sg - s)gL}\ ]/2(sg - s) \qquad [3.30]$$

It is often possible to reduce the form given in equation 3.30 to a substantively interpretable expression. Unfortunately, that is not the case in this instance. We can apply this formula to the results obtained for Essex County earlier. Using the values for the parameters when $L = 1$ (equation 3.22) and substituting into equation 3.30 we have

$$\hat{M}^* = [(.05) \pm \sqrt{(.05)^2 - 4(-.45)(.16)}\ ]/2(-.45) \qquad [3.31]$$

which reduces to

$$\hat{M}^* = [.05 \pm \sqrt{.2905}\ ]/(-.9) \qquad [3.32]$$

$$\hat{M}^* = 0.54,\ -0.66$$

Since M_t substantively represents a proportion of the population that has the political attitude, or has the disease, or belongs to a political party, and so forth, we are interested in values of M^* that lie in the $(0,1)$ interval. Values for M^* greater than 1 or less than 0 have no real-world interpretation for this model.

In the case of Essex County we find $\hat{M}^* = .54$. This means that when 54% of the voting population is mobilized in support of the Democratic party, gains and losses balance and the process is stationary unless perturbed by some external force. (It is important to note that M^* is a net state. The process continues at M^* but the level of mobilization stays the same, i.e., the process remains dynamic but the measure of the state—a number—no longer changes.)

Local Stability Analysis

A logical next question is: What happens when the process is disturbed by external forces? These may include short-run political forces such as political scandals, economic conditions, and international crises. These short-run forces would shock the system away from the equilibrium. After these forces have perturbed the political system, will the process converge toward the equilibrium point or will it diverge? We have solved the quadratic form to determine its equilibria, but we have not yet provided a means to test for stability.

For nonlinear dynamic equations stability can be local or global. Local stability means that, within some neighborhood of the equilibrium point, the process will converge toward the equilibrium point after it is perturbed. Global stability implies that the process is stable no matter what the perturbation (for a more complete description of stability see Rosen, 1970; May, 1974).

First we apply a technique to investigate local stability at the equilibrium points, and then we will take advantage of some general results of Chaundy and Phillips (1936), reworked by Sprague (1969), to determine global stability for this specific quadratic form. The technique used to investigate local stability has a wider application for more complex, nonlinear models.

An analysis of small perturbations around the equilibrium point M^* begins by writing the perturbed mobilization level as

$$\Delta M_t = M^* + X_t \qquad [3.33]$$

Here X_t measures a small disturbance to the equilibrium M^* within some specified neighborhood. Now X_t must obey the original laws of change for the mobilization process given by equation 3.6. However, in a small neighborhood of the equilibrium—X_t is a *small* perturbation—a basic result from the calculus of numerical analysis may be invoked. It is possible to represent the process by a particular transformation, and, with an additional trick justified by the assumption that the perturbation is small, characterize the behavior of the *nonlinear* equation as essentially *linear* in the neighborhood of the particular equilibrium point chosen. This procedure is called an expansion in a Taylor series.

An approximate difference equation for the perturbation measure is obtained by a Taylor expansion of the equation for our original model, equation 3.6, about the equilibrium point. The Taylor series expansion provides a linearization of the model because the linear term in the expansion dominates the series in a small neighborhood, and terms of order two and higher can be neglected. The expansion takes the following form

$$\Delta X_t = aX_t \qquad \text{or} \qquad X_{t+1} = (1 + a)X_t \qquad [3.34]$$

where a is the partial derivative of ΔM_t with respect to M_t evaluated at the equilibrium point M^* (obtained from equation 3.24). Hence,

$$a = [\partial(\Delta M_t)]/(\partial M_t) = 2(sg - s)M^* + sL - f - g - sgL \qquad [3.35]$$

It measures the mobilization growth rate in the immediate neighborhood of the equilibrium point.

Equation 3.34 is a first-order linear difference equation for which we have an explicit solution. It has the form

$$X_t = X_0(1 + a)^t \qquad [3.36]$$

where X_0 is the initial small perturbation. The disturbance dies away if $(1 + a)$ lies in the open interval $(-1, +1)$, diverges if $(1 + a) > 1$ or $(1 + a) \leqslant -1$, and is constant if $(1 + a) = 1$. Thus the neighborhood stability analysis of the equilibrium point M^* shows the point to be stable if and only $-1 < (1 + a) < +1$, or more simply, $-2 < a < 0$.

Applying these results to our empirical example, the mobilization of the Democratic party in Essex County, substitute equation 3.35 into equation 3.34 to obtain

$$\Delta X_t = [2(sg - s)M^* + sL - f - g - sgL]X_t \qquad [3.37]$$

Disaggregating ΔX_t gives

$$X_{t+1} = [1 + 2(sg - s)M^* + sL - f - g - sgL]X_t \qquad [3.38]$$

where

$$1 + a = [1 + 2(sg - s)M^* + sL - f - g - sgL] \qquad [3.39]$$

Evaluating the coefficient of X_t at $M^* = 0.54$ using the estimates for the parameters s, f, g, and L from equation 3.22 gives

$$(1 + a) = (1 - .49 - .05) = 0.46 \qquad [3.40]$$

Since $1 + a = .46$ and therefore lies in the (0.1) interval, we know that the disturbance is monotonically convergent and dies out. This means that the equilibrium $M^* = 0.54$ for Essex County is locally stable. The mobilization of the Democratic party converges toward .54 of the voting population, which is a locally stable equilibrium (this discussion is adapted from May, 1974).

Global Stability Analysis for Quadratic Recursive Forms

In general there are no techniques for investigating global stability for nonlinear models. We can investigate local stability by linearizing the model with Taylor series expansions around the equilibrium points, but this only provides stability analyses in the small area. There are, however, some general results for a particular nonlinear form, the quadratic, reported by Chaundy and Phillips (1936) and further explicated by Sprague (1969). Chaundy and Phillips consider a difference equation of the following form:

$$M_{t+1} = AM_t^2 + BM_t + C \qquad [3.41]$$

where A, B, and C are real numbers independent of t. We can immediately see that our model is isomorphic to this form. Chaundy and Phillips do not provide an explicit solution, but conditions of convergence, divergence, and ultimate qualitative behavior can be developed from their discussion. Only a few of the results are presented here; the inquisitive reader should consult the original source.

First define a quantity K by

$$K = [-1 \pm \sqrt{1 + 4[(B/2)^2 - B/2 - AC]}]/-2 \qquad [3.42]$$

where A, B, and C are from equation 3.41. This produces three possibilities: two real and unequal Ks, two real and equal Ks, or a pair of complex Ks. Six cases are considered below.

Case 1. If K given by equation 3.42 is complex, then the process is divergent, diverging to infinity.

If K is real, choose that K that is $\geq .5$. One of the Ks should meet this condition.

Case 2. If $|AM_0 + B/2| > K$, then the process M_t diverges to infinity.

Case 3. If $|AM_0 + B/2| = K$, then the process M_t is stationary. This does not mean the process will converge if displaced.

Case 4. If $|AM_0 + B/2| < K$ and $1/2 \leq K \leq 3/2$, then the process M_t converges to a value

$$M^* = (1 - K - B/2)/A \qquad [3.43]$$

The limit M^* is dependent on A, B, and C since K depends on C. Convergence in this case is monotonic if $1/2 \leq K \leq 1$.

Case 5. If $|AM_0 + B/2| < K$ and $3/2 \leq K \leq 2$, then the process M_t oscillates finitely.

Case 6. If $|AM_0 + B/2| < K$ and $K > 2$, then the process M_t diverges to infinity with a certain exception, i.e., if M_0 is chosen so that the expression $|AM_0 + B/2|$ is an element of a set involving the square roots of the expression $K^2 - K$, then the process M_t oscillates finitely (this discussion is based on results from Sprague, 1969). Given particular estimates of any quadratic form, we may deduce its qualitative behavior over time.

We now apply these conditions for convergence to the data on Democratic mobilization for Essex County. We have already determined that there is a locally stable equilibrium at $M^* = .54$. We now take advantage of the preceding results to see if the locally stable equilibrium satisfies the Chaundy/Phillips conditions for global stability. First the real numbers A, B, and C are defined

$$A = m_2 = sg - s$$

$$B = m_1 = 1 + sL - f - g - sgL$$

$$C = m_0 = gL \qquad\qquad [3.44]$$

Substituting the estimates for the parameters for s, f, g, and L for Essex County from equation 3.22 into the formulas in equation 3.44, we obtain the values A = -.45, B = .95, and C = .16. Using these values we calculate K as follows

$$K = [-1 \pm \sqrt{1 + 4(.23 - .475 + .07)}\,]/-2$$

$$K = .78, .23 \qquad\qquad [3.45]$$

We choose .78 as the value for K and find that Case 4 applies. Now examine the value $|AM_0 + B/2|$. Substituting values for A and B we obtain $|.45M_0 + .475|$. The condition for convergence of the process is

$$|-.45M_0 + .475| < .78 \qquad\qquad [3.46]$$

The inequality 3.46 emphasizes that *convergence for nonlinear difference equations is dependent upon initial conditions.* Thus the starting point of the mobilization process is an important consideration in the determination of long run limiting behavior. For what values of M_0 does inequality 3.46 hold? We begin by looking at the extreme values for M_0. Here, if inequality 3.46 holds for the extreme values, then it holds for all values of M_0. M_0 can range across the (0,1) interval. Both extreme values 0 and 1 for M_0 satisfy the inequality thus any permissible starting value satisfies the condition for convergence. We also note that convergence of the process is monotonic since K lies in the (1/2,1) interval. Finally, M* calculated using equation 3.43 equals .54 for Essex County. This is the same value obtained using the quadratic formula, which is as it should be.

Summary

We have investigated the mathematical properties of the first-order quadratic difference equation used to model mobilization processes characterized by diffusion or contagion. Although explicit solutions for the quadratic are not available, the quadratic can be solved for equilibrium points using the quadratic formula. Local stability was investigated using a Taylor series expansion around the equilibrium point. But this provides information about stability only in the small, in some neighborhood of a particular equilibrium. In general, for nonlinear models, local stability can be investigated using this technique. Unfortunately, the technique is of limited usefulness since the exact size of the neighborhood is usually unknown.

Thus, while one can easily determine *local* dynamics, it is much more difficult to obtain a global picture of the dynamic landscape of nonlinear systems. This, of course, is not the case with linear models, since neighborhood analyses describe global dynamics as well. In nonlinear systems, however, we do not know what will happen if the system is disturbed with sufficient force: The states may return toward equilibrium, move into a stable limit cycle, or explode to infinity. The qualitative behavior will, in fact, depend upon the second- and higher-order terms of the Taylor expansion, which are discarded in a neighborhood analysis. Fortunately, in the case of the quadratic, some general results are known. Conditions for convergence and divergence were reported and are applicable for all models that take this form. In this particular instance, then, a partial global analysis *is* possible.

We continue our treatment of dynamic models in Chapter 4 by returning to linear difference equations, but we extend our consideration to systems of interdependent equations.

4. LINEAR SYSTEMS AND HIGHER-ORDER EQUATIONS: ARMS RACES AND FEEDBACK PROCESSES

In previous chapters our development of discrete-time models is limited to single first-order equations. This chapter extends our consideration to higher-order models. Two different models are developed: the Richardson arms race model and a feedback model of legislative review. The two-nation, linear arms race model can be reduced, for analytic purposes, to a linear, second-order difference equation with constant coefficients, and the feedback model treats single-equation, higher-order lag processes more generally. During the course of this chapter a matrix representation of the arms race model is presented, some useful analytic approaches are explored, and general solution strategies for linear models or linear systems of higher order are outlined.

Higher-Order Models

Any social science model, whether it is dynamic or static, mathematical or verbal, serves as an abstraction of reality that necessarily simplifies the subject of study. A first-order dynamic model simplifies time dependence by expressing a current system state as a simple or complex function of the immediately preceding system state, ignoring that state's extended history. The reality is clearly more complex than the abstraction. Given a system state at t, we might reasonably extend the functional form indefinitely back in time so that:

$$S_t = f(\Sigma S_{t-k}) \qquad k = 1, 2, 3, \ldots \qquad [4.1]$$

Econometricians have developed statistical technologies for identifying the structure of such time-ordered dependence. These statistical techniques are useful as an inductive exercise in model building—as a way to develop substantive ideas regarding the nature of time dependence and system memory. A theoretical model, however, as it is understood in this monograph, is properly seen as a direct mathematical expression of a substantive idea. Thus, it is an inappropriate modeling strategy to extend the structure of temporal dependence simply to be safe, or simply because the data are available. The structure of time dependence ultimately must be specified on the basis of a theoretical understanding of the phenomenon in question. In many instances this means that a first-order model must be discarded in favor of a higher-order model. For example, in the mobilization models of the previous chapters it might be appropriate to argue that recently recruited individuals (those recruited in the last time period, $t - 1$) have different defection rates than individuals with longer membership histories (those recruited at $t - 2$ and before). This would imply two loss rate hypotheses and a second-order process.

Higher-order models can also be developed on the basis of two or more separate, but functionally interdependent, statements of change. These component parts may be first-order specifications: Two interdependent first-order models produce a second-order system, three interdependent first-order models imply a third-order system, and so forth (Samuelson, 1974). The Richardson arms race model developed in this chapter is written as two first-order equations that produce higher-order reduced forms (a single equation of order two for each system state). Thus, in introducing second-order models the concept of linear interdependence of system states is also introduced.

The Richardson Arms Race Model

Lewis F. Richardson's model of arms races (1960) initiated a wide spectrum of dynamic modeling concerning the causes of war and armaments buildups (see Gillespie and Zinnes, 1977). Richardson formulated his model as a continuous-time process utilizing linear differential equations. We present his argument in discrete time by utilizing linear difference equations. The model portrays the interdependent armaments behavior of two or more nations, and identifies three factors that determine armament levels: (1) the economic burden created by maintaining existing levels of military preparedness, (2) a nation's response to the threat presented by other nations and their armament levels, and (3) the grievances, ambitions, and prejudices that are unique to the internal politics of each nation. The model for a single nation interacting with another single nation is written in the following form:

$$\Delta X_t = kY_t - aX_t + g \qquad [4.2]$$

where:

X_t = the armament level in nation X at year t

Y_t = the armament level in nation Y at year t

a = the economic burden experienced by nation X in attempting to maintain its armament level

k = the threat felt by nation X due to the armament level of nation Y

g = the effect of ambitions, prejudices, and hostilities upon the armament level of nation X

In words, nation X will modify its arms level from time t to t + 1 as follows: It will examine the arms level of its enemy, and (disregarding other considerations) respond by building new arms at rate k. Nation X will also consider the costs of maintaining its current armaments (X_t), and reduce its arms levels at rate a on the basis of its own perceived economic constraints. Finally, purely domestic considerations—aggressiveness, nationalism, pacifism, patriotism—create pressures to increase (or decrease) armaments by an amount g independently of what nation Y is doing. It is the net effect of these three considerations that produces the change (positive or negative) in X_t.

Simultaneously, nation Y makes similar decisions regarding its own future armament levels according to the same rules. With only minor modification, the armament behavior of nation Y can be expressed as:

$$\Delta Y_t = k'X_t - a'Y_t + g' \qquad\qquad [4.3]$$

where:

a′ = the economic burden experienced by nation Y in attempting to maintain its armament level

k′ = the threat felt by nation Y due to the armament level of nation X

g′ = the effect of ambitions, prejudices, and hostilities upon the armament level of nation Y

Notice that k, k′, a, and a′ are all *rates* or proportions, while g and g′ are both *levels* measured in the same metric as X_t and Y_t.

Clearly, nations X and Y are locked in an *interdependent system* defined by equations 4.2 and 4.3. Furthermore, this system is simultaneous in its timing. Interdependence and simultaneity are typical of many social processes: The behavior of a first actor depends on the behavior of a second actor and vice versa. Game theory is one well-known approach to analyzing such conflict situations, but dynamic models are also powerful tools for examining them.

Arriving at a Second-Order Reduced Form

The two-nation model is composed of two equations (4.2 and 4.3) that are both first order, but the equations are clearly interdependent. Neither of the first-order equations can be translated into the recursive form solved in Chapter 2 because both have exogenous system states on the right-hand side. In order to explore the dynamics of the system represented by these equations, we translate them into a different form. First, by disaggregating the change operator, Δ, and advancing equation 4.2 one time unit, we produce:

$$X_{t+2} = (1 - a)X_{t+1} + kY_{t+1} + g \qquad [4.4]$$

Algebraic substitution of equation 4.3 into equation 4.4 yields:

$$X_{t+2} = (1 - a)X_{t+1} + k[(1 - a')Y_t + k'X_t + g'] + g \qquad [4.5]$$

Our goal is to express X_t as a function of previous X_{t-k} alone, but equation 4.5 still contains Y_t on the right-hand side. Rearranging equation 4.2 produces:

$$Y_t = [X_{t+1} - (1 - a)X_t - g]/k \qquad [4.6]$$

Finally, by substituting equation 4.6 into equation 4.5 and algebraically rearranging the result, we arrive at our goal.

$$X_{t+2} = (2 - a - a')X_{t+1} + (kk' - 1 + a + a' - aa')X_t + kg' + ga' \qquad [4.7]$$

The armament behavior of nation X is now expressed solely as a function of its own previous armament levels, even though the original theoretical model clearly recognizes the interdependence between nations X and Y. The price of obtaining an analytic form for the behavior of X_t that is not *explicitly* dependent on Y_t is an increase in the order of the lag structure for the new recursive form. That increased time lag *implicitly* captures the interdependence of the original system. With appropriate rearrangement, equations 4.2 and 4.3 can also be used to express the armament behavior of nation Y in a recursive form:

$$Y_{t+2} = (2 - a - a')Y_{t+1} + (k'k - 1 + a + a' - a'a)Y_t + k'g - g'a \qquad [4.8]$$

Putting the Arms Race in Matrix Notation

The arms race model is easily expanded to accommodate interrelationships between more than two nations. The notation for the multination model quickly becomes burdensome, however. Just as a two-nation arms race produces a second-order system, an arms race with n nations produces a system of order n. A more convenient expression for such a system makes use of matrix algebra.

A matrix generalization is most easily accomplished (and made extraordinarily useful) if it is recognized that the operation of taking a first difference ($\Delta X_t = X_{t+1} - X_t$) defines a *linear* operation. Thus, delta (Δ) is a linear operator, and *for many purposes* it may be treated algebraically as an ordinary constant. The theory of linear operators is part of operational mathematics (Churchill, 1972) and is developed for the discrete-time case by Goldberg (1958) among others. Most techniques for solving linear differential or difference equations rely on operational methods using, respectively, the Laplace and the so-called z-transform. In probability theory these methods arise when generating moments of a probability distribution. All that is used here, we reiterate, is the basic fact that the operator delta may be treated as an algebraic quantity.

Rewrite equations 4.2 and 4.3 as a simultaneous system

$$\Delta X_t = -aX_t + kY_t + g$$

$$\Delta Y_t = -a'Y_t + k'X_t + g' \qquad [4.9]$$

Next move the *state* variables (X_t and Y_t) to the left-hand side, obtaining

$$(\Delta + a)X_t \qquad - kY_t = g$$

$$-k'X_t + (\Delta + a')Y_t = g' \qquad [4.10]$$

Our strategy at this point, which is perfectly general for the n by n case, is to detach the coefficients of the state variables as a matrix and to write the state variables and the right-hand side quantities as vectors. Thus, write

$$\begin{pmatrix} (\Delta + a) & -k \\ -k' & (\Delta + a') \end{pmatrix} \begin{pmatrix} X_t \\ Y_t \end{pmatrix} = \begin{pmatrix} g \\ g' \end{pmatrix} \qquad [4.11]$$

which expresses our *system in matrix form*. Pursuing our plan of treating the "Δ" as a constant we may invoke rules of matrix algebra and solve for system states X_t and Y_t. Readers familiar with matrix algebra may wish to solve equation 4.11 for system states at this point. Readers less familiar with matrix techniques are directed to the Appendix where we find the solution using Cramer's rule.

Finding the System Equilibrium

Even without matrix operations, the equilibrium point in a two dimensional (X,Y) plane is readily obtained using the system in equation 4.9 and simple algebraic manipulations. Replace ΔX_t and ΔY_t with 0 to denote a steady state, and replace X_t and Y_t with X* and Y* to denote the unique equilibrium point that produces the steady state.

$$0 = -aX^* + kY^* + g$$

$$0 = -a'Y^* + k'X^* + g' \qquad [4.12]$$

In order to solve for X^*, isolate Y^* on the left-hand side of both equations in the system.

$$-Y^* = -(a/k)X^* + (g/k)$$

$$Y^* = (k'/a')X^* + (g'/a') \qquad [4.13]$$

Adding the two equations together and algebraically rearranging the result gives the equilibrium for X:

$$X^* = \frac{ga' + g'k}{aa' - kk'} \qquad [4.14]$$

Parallel procedures produce the equilibrium value for Y:

$$Y^* = \frac{gk' + g'a}{aa' - kk'} \qquad [4.15]$$

Note that while equations 4.14 and 4.15 give equilibrium values for X and Y, the *system* is in equilibrium only when both X_t and Y_t are *simultaneously* at equilibrium. We thus denote the equilibrium for the system as the point (X^*, Y^*).

The system equilibrium (X^*, Y^*) defines that point in the two-dimensional state space of the system such that, if chosen as initial conditions, successive state values are numerically equal. In substantive terms this point describes the constant arms levels characteristic of two nations in the steady state—two nations that have achieved a balance of power. For a *stable* system, both nations *return* to this equilibrium after a short-term exogenous shock moves them away from it. Thus, the substantive significance of equilibrium depends upon stability, and determinations regarding stability are readily made using the solution to the second-order reduced forms of equations 4.7 and 4.8.

Solutions for Higher-Order Systems

We detail a solution technique for higher-order linear equations based on the second-order arms race model, but the same strategy applies to systems of arbitrary order. The desire for a closed-form solution is motivated by two deductive, analytic questions: First, under what conditions will the equilibrium be stable? Second, what will be the qualitative nature of the path approaching (or diverging from) equilibrium? For the case of linear difference equations, even without constant coefficients, solutions exist and are unique once an appropriate number of initial conditions are specified. The only remaining issue is finding such a solution, and that is our next task.

In our development of higher-order solutions we rely on a general theorem for systems of linear difference equations. This theorem asserts that the general solution for a difference equation is the sum of *any* particular solution and the general solution for the homogeneous form (Goldberg, 1958). In order to apply this theorem, a recursive form difference equation of arbitrary order is rewritten with all states and state lags on the left-hand side, and all other terms on the right-hand side. The problem is then broken down into two parts: (1) finding *any* solution for this complete equation and (2) finding the general solution for the homogeneous equation, i.e., for the complete equation with zero right-hand side. In order to fix these ideas we first demonstrate this solution strategy for the first-order linear equation with constant coefficients that was previously solved in Chapter 2.[5]

Consider the first-order equation in its recursive form

$$Y_{t+1} = a_0 + a_1 Y_t \qquad [4.16]$$

This may be placed in *canonical form* as the *complete* equation

$$Y_{t+1} - a_1 Y_t = a_0 \qquad [4.17]$$

with the associated *homogeneous equation*

$$Y_{t+1} - a_1 Y_t = 0 \qquad [4.18]$$

From earlier developments (see Chapter 2) we know that one particular solution to the complete equation 4.17 is the equilibrium solution:

$$Y^* = a_0/(1 - a_1) \qquad [4.19]$$

Now consider the homogeneous equation 4.18. In order to apply the theorem, a *general solution* must also be obtained for this homogeneous form. We exhibit such a solution and refer the reader to Goldberg (1958) for proofs that such solutions always exist, and that they are unique once initial conditions are supplied.

We attempt to find a solution for equation 4.18 among the simplest functions and suppose that

$$Y_t = r^t \qquad [4.20]$$

may work. Substituting equation 4.20 into equation 4.18 yields

$$r^{t+1} - a_1 r^t = 0 \qquad [4.21]$$

which, when divided by r' (for $r' \neq 0$) gives, on rearrangement, $r = a_1$.

In order to allow for different initial conditions, a constant that varies with initial conditions somehow must be introduced. Try a simple multiplicative c. If a_1^t is a solution to equation 4.18, is it also true that ca_1^t is a solution? The reader should substitute and see that ca_1^t is indeed a solution. In fact, it is the general unique solution with c an arbitrary constant to be determined by initial conditions.

According to the theorem, the solutions to equations 4.17 and 4.18 may be combined additively to arrive at the general complete solution. We try obtaining

$$Y_t = Y^* + ca_1^t \qquad [4.22]$$

Suppose an initial condition is Y_0. Then we have

$$Y_0 = Y^* + ca_1^0 \qquad [4.23]$$

which implies

$$c = (Y_0 - Y^*) \qquad [4.24]$$

Thus equation 4.22, our solution, may be written as

$$Y_t = Y^* + (Y_0 - Y^*)a_1^t \qquad [4.25]$$

and this is seen to be precisely the result shown in equation 2.43 of Chapter 2. But note, the current result was obtained by applying a *general theorem* applicable to linear equations of arbitrary order. The procedure just exhibited will work in all such cases although the algebraic effort is frequently onerous.

Recall that the recursive form results for the two-state Richardson's model. It is evident from the development leading up to those results that the *homogeneous equation* is the same for both states—a general property of nth-order linear systems. Furthermore, particular solutions for the state equations have already been obtained. They are simply the equilibrium values for the respective states—X^* and Y^*. Hence, to apply the strategy of the theorem, our only task is to solve *one* homogeneous equation. That equation is, for state X_t,

$$X_{t+2} + (a + a' - 2)X_{t+1} + (1 + aa' - kk' - a - a')X_t = 0 \qquad [4.26]$$

Let

$$b = a + a' - 2,$$

$$c = 1 + aa' - kk' - a - a'$$

and

Z_i = either X_i or Y_i

Our problem may then be recast as finding the general solution for

$$Z_{i+2} + bZ_{i+1} + cZ_i = 0 \qquad [4.27]$$

Proceed as before and try r^i. Substitution and division by r^i yields

$$r^2 + br + c = 0 \qquad [4.28]$$

Equation 4.28 is recognized as a polynomial in r of order two—the quadratic. It is frequently referred to as the *characteristic equation* of the system. Evidently, either root of the quadratic will satisfy equation 4.27 and, as before, we multiply each by a constant to allow for the two sequential initial conditions required by the general theory. Thus, assuming the roots of equation 4.28 are real and unequal, the solution to equation 4.27 may be written as

$$Z_i = Z^* + c_1 r_1^i + c_2 r_2^i \qquad [4.29]$$

Equation 4.29 may be used to determine the values of the constants given initial conditions Z_0 and Z_1. The appropriate relations are

$$c_1 = Z_0 - Z^* - c_2$$
$$c_2 = (Z_1 - Z^*)/(r_2 - r_1) - [r_1(Z_0 - Z^*)]/(r_2 - r_1)$$
$$= \frac{(Z_1 - Z^*) - r_1(Z_0 - Z^*)}{r_2 - r_1} \qquad [4.30]$$

Note that the *form* of the solution in equation 4.29 is similar to the *form* of the solution shown in equation 4.22 except that an extra root and constant occur. This is general: One new root will be added along with the new constant for each increment in the order of the system.

Before turning to the analytic potential of this solution, two additional complications must be considered. First, it may be that the solution will have only one (repeated) root. Second, it may be that the roots are imaginary, in which case they occur as complex conjugate pairs. For present purposes note that these cases are technically manageable, leading to unique solutions that exist in the real domain. If the roots are complex then the solution contains a trigonometric function that supplies an oscillatory motion to the states of the system with period longer than two.

The most important fact about these potential difficulties, however, is that *they exhaust the possibilities.* Fundamental mathematical theorems provide assurance that the roots of a characteristic equation with co-efficients that lie in the real-number domain will produce roots that are either: (1) unique and real, (2) repeated and real, or (3) complex conjugates with a trigonometric real representation.

Extracting the roots of characteristic equations with order greater than two may be a time-consuming task in numerical analysis (Hamming, 1971). Fortunately, the solution *form* can be used to obtain a set of criteria for determining stability expressed solely in terms of inequalities involving coefficients of the *homogeneous* equation (May, 1974; Samuelson, 1974). Less fortunately, if the qualitative nature of the approach toward (or departure from) equilibrium is to be determined, it is necessary to know whether the roots of the solution are real, complex, and (or) repeated. Knowing the motion in the system requires solving the characteristic equation for its roots, and this may be hard work if the system is at all large, requiring numerical approximation techniques and a high-speed computer.

Putting the Solution to Work

Inspection of equation 4.29 casts light on both the quality of time paths and convergence. Clearly, for the case of real roots, all roots must be less than one in absolute value if the process is to approach the limiting or equilibrium value Z^*. If one (or both) of the real roots is negative then the time path of the system state, whether converging or diverging, will oscillate with period two. If the roots are complex conjugates, then a single quantity can be developed for the roots which depends on the real and imaginary parts of the quadratic solution. This quantity—the modulus of the roots in the complex plane—must be less than unity if the process is to be convergent. For the case of complex roots we also know, as indicated above, that the time path of the states will be trigonometric with period greater than two.[6]

Which case obtains is dependent, of course, on the particular parameter value assignments chosen, determined, or estimated. In the case of the linear arms race model the characteristic roots determined by the quadratic formula are

$$r_1, r_2 = \frac{b^2}{2} \pm \frac{\sqrt{b^2 - 4c}}{2} \qquad [4.31]$$

But, on the basis of the equalities shown under equation 4.26, we can write, after some simplification,

$$r_1, r_2 = \frac{(a + a' - 2)^2}{2} \pm \frac{\sqrt{(a - a')^2 + 4kk'}}{2} \qquad [4.32]$$

Thus, trigonometric motion will result if

$$(a - a')^2 + 4kk' < 0 \qquad [4.33]$$

which simplifies to

$$4kk' < -[(a - a')^2] \qquad [4.34]$$

In words, long-run oscillation of armament levels depends on the relationship of the system parameters attached to system states—a nation's own economic condition and its fear of an opponent's armament—but does not depend on internal grievances (the g and g' terms). But the deductive consequence arising from the *form* of inequality 4.34 is stronger. If k, k', a, and a' are all greater than zero (which must be true if the model is to have its intended interpretation), then the left-hand side of inequality 4.34 is always positive, while the right-hand side is *at most* zero.[7] Thus, *long-period oscillation is impossible* given the logical structure of the model. The natural next question is: Does the model also rule out short-term (period two) oscillation? Period two oscillations will arise provided the term

$$(a + a' - 2) - \sqrt{(a - a')^2 + 4kk'} < 0 \qquad [4.35]$$

This condition does not preclude period two oscillation on a priori or logical grounds because inequality 4.35 can be satisfied if internal economic strains are sufficiently small and perceived dangers sufficiently large.

Thus, the formalism leads to deductive conclusions that have clear substantive interpretations. And these deductively obtained conclusions offer an alternative means for empirical investigation and analysis. Rather than calculating measures of statistical fit or correspondence, the investigator might compare the qualities of real-world arms races to the arms races that are predicted on the basis of the hypothesized model. In short, an adequate model should reproduce the qualities of an observed social process.

Stability Conditions

Goldberg (1958: 171-172) develops necessary and sufficient stability conditions for the second-order difference equation:

Condition I: $1 + b + c > 1$

Substituting the Richardson model coefficients yields

$$1 + a + a' - 2 + 1 + aa' - kk' - a - a' > 0$$

which simplifies to

$$aa' > kk' \qquad [4.36]$$

Condition II: $\quad 1 - b + c > 0$

Substitution yields

$$1 - a - a' + 2 + 1 + aa' - kk' - a - a' > 0$$

which simplifies to

$$4 - 2a - 2a' + aa' > kk' \qquad [4.37]$$

Condition III: $\quad 1 - c > 0$

Again substitution and simplification yield

$$kk' + a + a' > aa' \qquad [4.38]$$

Now, it can be readily shown that as long as the four model parameters (a, a', k, k') lie within the $(0,1)$ interval, the conditions in inequalities 4.37 and 4.38 must be satisfied. We have already argued that the parameters must be positive, and two examples show that it is entirely reasonable that we expect them to be less than one: Armaments for nation X are not likely to (1) increase by more than nation Y's armament level due to threat alone or (2) decrease to a negative value due to economic burden alone.

Thus, we are left with one important substantive condition for a stable system—inequality 4.36: The product of the nations' economic strain must exceed the product of the nations' mutual fear. That is, as long as the interaction between two nations' economic distress surpasses the inter-action between their fears of each other, then their armaments race converges toward equilibrium. In substantive terms, a balance of power results. If the interaction between the economic strain of the two nations is less than the interaction between their mutual fears, then the arms race diverges.

The Geometry of Stability: An Alternative Approach

A direct geometric interpretation for stability conditions that provides additional insight into the arms race process can be obtained. This geometry is especially useful for the common and both substantively and theoretically important case of a two-state system, such as that portrayed by the classic Richardson model. This form of analysis may be developed for both linear and nonlinear systems, and in Chapter 5 we apply it to the analysis of a nonlinear system. The reader should view our development as useful in its own right for linear models, but preparatory for the non-linear case in which solutions in closed form are frequently elusive, and geometric reasoning thus assumes, necessarily, a more prominent analytic role.

The condition for application of this technology is that, except for system states, time does not occur *explicitly* in the change equations. In particular, any input must be treated as a fixed parameter for purposes of analyzing equilibrium behavior. This allows us to develop an analytic technique for studying the system with time eliminated, and hence with analytic attention focused (where it should be) on the interaction between states. Such a system (with explicit dependence on time removed) is referred to in the literature as an autonomous system.

The geometric strategy is to represent the behavior of the system in a plane where one axis represents one system state and a second axis represents the other system state. In the case of our two-nation arms race model the geometric representation, then, is the state space of the (X,Y) plane. The placement of system states on abscissa and ordinate is arbitrary, and we shall place Y on the ordinate and X on the abscissa. The goal of this geometric portrait in the state space is to provide a graphical means for (1) determining or locating equilibria and (2) understanding the motion of the system in the neighborhood of the equilibrium.

Consider the original arms race model, specified in equations 4.2 and 4.3.

$$\Delta X_t = -aX_t + kY_t + g$$

$$\Delta Y_t = -a'Y_t + k'X_t + g'$$

This system is already in autonomous form (because no parameter is directly time dependent), and hence the system is ready for analysis as written.

The system is at equilibrium when there is no longer system change: The quantitative measures of system states maintain constant numeric values through time ($\Delta X_t = \Delta Y_t = 0$). Thus, at equilibrium in X, equation 4.2 may be written as:

$$kY_t = aX_t - g \qquad [4.39]$$

and, provided k does not equal zero, rewritten as

$$Y_t = (a/k)X_t - g/k \qquad [4.40]$$

Note that Y is expressed as a function of X and fixed parameters with time are suppressed. The form of the function is a straight line, and it is an easy matter to plot this slope-intercept form in the state space plane (X,Y). This plot is exhibited in Figure 4.1, giving the locus of points in X and Y that produces a *steady state in X*—a numeric level in state X that is not

58

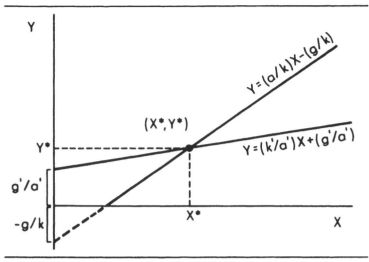

Figure 4.1 Phase Plane Representation of Equilibrium in a Two-Nation Arms Race

changing. Similarly, at equilibrium in Y, equation 4.3 may be written as

$$Y = (k'/a')X + g'/a' \qquad [4.41]$$

This locus of points in the (X,Y) plane is satisfied when *state Y* is not changing in *numeric value*. Both loci are plotted in Figure 4.1.

The geometry of Figure 4.1 is worth careful study. As long as the two loci are not wholly coincidental, there is *at most one point* that satisfies both equation 4.40 and equation 4.41, and this point is the system equilibrium. Furthermore, there will almost certainly be an equilibrium *for the entire system* since the likelihood of parallel loci with different intercepts must be very small. Finally, different slopes produce different values for the system equilibrium (X^*,Y^*), and these values might be outside the first quadrant, giving a substantive interpretation that cannot be empirically attained. (The first quadrant is unique in that it provides values for X and Y that are positive—a substantive necessity.) This supplies a nice example of mathematical existence not matching empirical possibility. Under our assumption that all parameters are positive, it is clear geometrically that the condition for the existence of a positive equilibrium—an equilibrium in the first quadrant—is given by

$$k'/a' < a/k \qquad [4.42]$$

And, algebraic manipulation of inequality 4.42 produces an interesting result:

$$kk' < aa' \qquad [4.43]$$

which is identical to inequality 4.36, the stability condition for the model. Thus, the geometric analysis shows that if the process converges, and if g and g' are both positive, convergence will be toward a first-quadrant equilibrium—an equilibrium for which a real-world descriptive interpretation exists. Put another way, if the geometry in Figure 4.1 holds, producing a first-quadrant equilibrium, then the equilibrium is stable. Conversely, although a runaway arms race is possible in the model, it will not be associated with a stable first-quadrant equilibrium.

The *approach* to equilibrium can be studied with this geometric strategy by assigning initial conditions (for X_t and Y_t) and a set of parameter values, using the *original* specification of equations 4.2 and 4.3. On this basis a one-period movement on X and Y is computed, and this movement is expressed in the state space as a single vector arising from the separate X and Y movements. The tail of the vector is located at the arbitrary starting point (a pair of initial conditions not equal to the equilibrium values), with length and direction determined by the particular numerical assignments that are chosen or determined or estimated for the parameters and the initial conditions. This process is repeated, using the computed values for X and Y as new initial conditions and then repeated again, and again, as far as one pleases. The path built up in this fashion describes the manner in which the equilibrium is approached (or not approached) in the (X,Y) state space.

Two cases of great theoretical interest in the traditional analysis of arms races are (1) a runaway arms race (the future all people fear) and (2) a balance of power (the future we hope for as making the best of a bad situation). These cases can be displayed as trajectories in the state space by drawing a series of vectors following the procedure just outlined. We illustrate the hopeful future of a stable balance of power.

Suppose the following assignment of parameter values that satisfy convergence:

$$
\begin{array}{ll}
a = .6 & a' = .8 \\
k = .9 & k' = .4 \\
g = .1 & g' = .1
\end{array}
\qquad [4.44]
$$

Then,

$$
\hat{X}^* = 1.42
$$
$$
\hat{Y}^* = .83
\qquad [4.45]
$$

and the equations for the point loci in the (X,Y) plane are

$$
Y = .667X - .111
$$
$$
Y = .500X + .125
\qquad [4.46]
$$

Substituting the equation 4.44 parameter values into the characteristic equation and solving for the roots we obtain

$$r_1 = .788$$

$$r_2 = -.428 \qquad [4.47]$$

and hence the approach to the equilibrium should include a period-two oscillatory component. Does our procedure square with these analytic results?

Assume,

$$X_0 = 1 \neq X^*$$

$$Y_0 = 1 \neq Y^* \qquad [4.48]$$

and proceed. The results are plotted in Figure 4.2. The geometry is not very interesting but it shows that movement in the state space is toward the equilibrium value as predicted. When nonlinear models or less restrictive linear models are analyzed, the trajectories in the state space show more interesting patterns, i.e., display more complex motion. This becomes evident in the geometric analysis of the nonlinear models in the next chapter.

Feedback Time Delay as a Destabilizing Influence

In Chapter 2 a stable system is defined as a system generating a sequence that approaches equilibrium or returns toward equilibrium after a disturbance moves it away from equilibrium. An infinite range of models lies within the general class of stable systems, producing sequences that approach equilibrium in both simple and complex paths, with varying degrees of speed. Thus, in an informal sense, some stable systems are more "stable" than others, producing more rapid convergence in a more straightforward fashion. Time delay in feedback loops is an important source of these destabilizing influences, and in this section we consider its inhibiting effect upon smooth, rapid convergence toward equilibrium. Building upon a model by Sprague (1976), the process of legislative review is constructed to examine the consequences of extended feedback structures.

Let us imagine some government agency that makes a yearly trip to the legislature in order to secure funding. The bureaucratic leadership within the agency prepares a proposed agenda of undertakings, and this agenda, or demand, serves as a positive input into the process. (We define A_t as the activity of the agency at time t and U_t as the proposed agenda.) The legislature, usually an appropriations subcommittee, makes a deter-

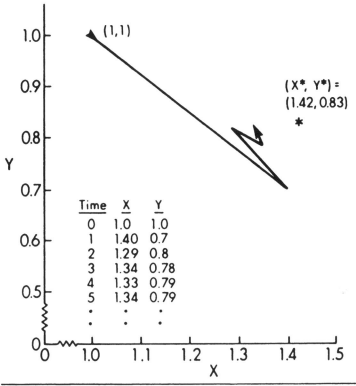

Figure 4.2 Phase Plane Representation of a First-Quadrant Approach Toward Equilibrium in a Two-Nation Arms Race

mination regarding the proposed agenda, and agrees to some proportion, α, accordingly. This part of the process can be written as:

$$A_t = \alpha U_t \qquad\qquad [4.49]$$

The legislature is not only concerned with the promise and potential of proposed activity, however, it is also concerned with past performance and past activity. Thus, at regular intervals a legislative oversight committee performs a review, and constrains future agency activity by eliminating inappropriate practices from the past. This review activity, and its subsequent recommendation, serves as negative feedback into the system. We denote this negative review or feedback parameter as β, and write the revised model as:

$$A_t = \alpha U_t - \beta A_{t-k} \qquad (k = 0, 1, 2, \ldots) \qquad [4.50]$$

This model is an admittedly crude characterization of the interaction between bureaucratic agencies and legislatures, but it serves to illustrate several features of the relationship between legislative review and system stability. The two parameters are separate and distinct parts of the process: α serves as an abstraction of the budgeting process and β as an abstraction of the oversight process. As any student of legislative politics knows, the budgeting process includes large doses of oversight activity, but legislative reform efforts at creating institutionalized mechanisms for policy oversight *outside* the budgeting process suggest the validity of an analytic separation between the two activities. (More realistic models of budgeting are developed in the next chapter.)

The time subscript for the review process is intentionally left undefined. By manipulating k we alter the time delay built into the oversight process. When k equals zero oversight is instantaneous, but as k grows larger the time correspondence between agency behavior and legislative review grows more attenuated.

Our goal is to observe the effect of this attentuation. In order to simplify our task, we hold α and β, as well as U_t, constant while varying k. As reasonable values for α and β, assume that our imaginary agency regularly wins approval for 75% of its proposed agenda of activities and regularly has 25% of its previous activity curtailed through the review process. To further simplify our task, think in terms of dollars: We measure A_t and U_t with a dollar metric, assuming that activity reductions and approvals proportionally translate into budgetary change. Further assume that the cost of the proposed agenda is constant: U_t equals 8 million dollars for all t. Finally, we trace agency history from three years before the instigation of the review procedure, where the three values for A_{t-3}, A_{t-2}, and A_{t-1} all equal 6 mllion dollars.

As a first scenario, consider the effect of instantaneous review, k = 0. Instantaneous review is produced in very specialized situations. Sprague (1976) suggests the example of forest fire appropriations, typically handled through supplemental appropriations due to the impossibility of adequately predicting the number and size of upcoming fires. We represent instantaneous review by setting k in equation 4.50 equal to zero and substituting values for α and β:

$$A_t = .75U_t - .25A_t = (.75/1.25)U_t \qquad [4.51]$$

Thus, given our constant input of an 8 million dollar budget request, the constant output of this process is 4.8 million dollars. More generally, instantaneous feedback produces a policy response proportional to demand or request, thereby tracking the demand smoothly and without delay.

As a second scenario, assume an annual review so that k = 1. This is typically the situation with a hard-working appropriations subcommittee in the U.S. Congress that performs a thorough review at the same time that it considers budget requests. The model becomes:

$$A_t = .75U_t - .25A_{t-1} \qquad [4.52]$$

This process, illustrated in Figure 4.3, is oscillatory with period two, converging toward a limit that also equals 4.8 million dollars.

By extending the time delay to two years, equation 4.50 becomes

$$A_t = .75U_t - .25A_{t-2} \qquad [4.53]$$

This form produces complex conjugate roots but is convergent, thereby creating a process with sinusoidal-like oscillations of decreasing magnitude[8] (see part B of Figure 4.3). Finally, by extending the time delay of review even farther so that k = 3, we produce the following specification,

$$A_t = .75U_t - .25A_{t-3} \qquad [4.54]$$

This time delay results in one negative root and two complex conjugate roots, producing a still more complicated time path (see part C of Figure 4.3).

Several comparisons among the three specifications shown in Figure 4.3 are noteworthy. As the time delay increases, the pattern of oscillation becomes more complex, and the amount of time required to approach equilibrium increases. That is, response time grows longer so that the system becomes less efficient. Second, the time delay has no effect on the equilibrium value for the system. Thus, by increasing the delay in review we increase the complexity of the short-run response, but we do not alter the steady-state response.

What have we learned from this exercise? Substantively, delays in legislative review can be expected to destabilize the policy process. The relationship between demand and response is most direct and unambiguous when legislative review is most immediate. If a legislature is going to exercise oversight, it should not drag its feet. More generally, time delay in feedback is destabilizing, if we accept the premise that a process with a complex, slow-responding time path is less stable than a process with a more direct and faster-responding time path.[9]

From a technical perspective such feedback arguments lead directly to single-equation models with characteristic equations of higher order. The general solution strategies illustrated for the Richardson's model are wholly applicable, and the reader might wish to choose a value for k in equation 4.50 and attempt a solution.

Summary

This chapter has introduced two substantive models: the Richardson arms race model and a feedback model of legislative review. These models illustrate the frequently occurring necessity of moving beyond first-order

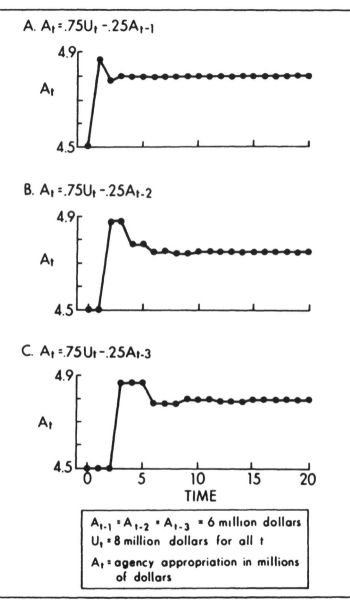

A. $A_t = .75U_t - .25A_{t-1}$

B. $A_t = .75U_t - .25A_{t-2}$

C. $A_t = .75U_t - .25A_{t-3}$

TIME

$A_{t-1} = A_{t-2} = A_{t-3} = 6$ million dollars
$U_t = 8$ million dollars for all t
$A_t =$ agency appropriation in millions of dollars

Figure 4.3 The Destabilizing Effects of Time Delays in Feedback

statements of change in depicting social and political processes. The solution procedures employed in this chapter are more demanding than those employed for the first-order model of Chapter 2, but the solutions for second-order models often provide useful analytic mileage. For models of order higher than two, substantively interpreting the solution is often quite difficult. As we saw in Chapter 3 and will see again in Chapter 5, some nonlinear models cannot be solved, but a number of alternative devices are available to exploit their analytic potential. In particular, geometric reasoning plays an especially important role in the two-state, nonlinear situation.

5. NONLINEAR DYNAMIC SYSTEMS: BUDGETARY COMPETITION

This chapter extends previously developed techniques to a consideration of the budgetary process. The mathematics of this chapter are somewhat more demanding because the model that we develop is a system of coupled nonlinear equations. Our goal is not to equip readers fully with the analytical methods required to conduct similar analyses, but rather to illustrate the direction in which the work in this monograph naturally moves.

The appropriations process is perhaps the most obvious and observable American political phenomenon that systematizes and institutionalizes the Lasswellian (1958) formulation of politics as "who gets what, when and how." The concern over who gets what in budgeting is the substantive problem of this chapter. This question is simply: What (or who) determines how the allocation of resources to various budgetary players changes over time?

The presentation here focuses on agencies competing for federal funds. The model that is developed, however, illustrates a very general process: competition over limited resources. The logic of players (species, politicians, interest groups, fads) competing for a limited set of resources (food, votes, favors, members) has quite broad application. The generality may be further extended if we allow "predator/prey" interactions in addition to pure competition. In such systems, for example, the Lotka-Volterra models (May, 1974), one species grows but may be preyed upon by other species. Social analogs are obvious.

Incrementalism

In the area of budgeting one answer to "who gets what" has been termed the "theory of budgetary incrementalism." This theoretical approach to budgeting derives from studies of public administration and policymaking beginning, perhaps, with Simon's analysis of limited rationality in human decision making (1957).

Davis, Dempster, and Wildavsky (1966) were the first to formalize the incrementalist argument, which had been previously supported in other qualitative research (e.g., Fenno, 1966; Wildavsky, 1979). According to their formulation, this year's budget is determined by the level of last year's budget plus some increment. Interpretations of this increment vary—some suggest it is an inflation factor, others that it is due to the inherent nature of a bureaucracy to grow, some that it is merely a descriptive "as if" theory—but these alternative interpretations are not critical to our consideration. The model that seems to best express the incremental theory is:

$$\Delta Appro_t = \alpha(Appro_t) + error \qquad [5.1]$$

or, in more obviously *incremental* form, appropriations next year for an agency are given by *all* of last year's appropriation *plus* an augmentation or growth percentage. Hence, write symbolically

$$Appro_{t+1} = (1 + \alpha)Appro_t + error \qquad [5.2]$$

The formalization asserts that the change in any particular agency's appropriations, in dollars, is some constant proportion, α (its "fair share"), over its current level of funding (its "base"), plus some randomly distributed error from short-run political and economic forces. Note that the process is *linear with constant coefficients, first-order*, and *independent* of similar budgeting processes for other agencies, departments, or programs.

In empirical analyses, α is usually estimated between .05 and .10, with good agreement between observed and theoretically predicted values.[10] Indeed, this model and simple variants on it have been utilized to demonstrate budgetary incrementalism at the federal, state, and local levels and in the budgetary processes of other political systems (Wildavsky, 1975).

Notice two consequences of the formalization: (1) There is no equilibrium point for the process, and (2) the dynamics are inherently unstable, predicting geometric growth in appropriations over time. These consequences may be overlooked if all one desires is a short-term approximation of the dynamic process. The model fails, however, as a descriptively adequate statement of the logic underlying the process.

The incremental models of the budgeting process assume (1) constant marginal growth and (2) independence in outcomes for each budgetary player. In times when budgetary resources are limited, however, it may be more appropriate to treat budgeting as a competitive (not incremental) process with interdependent (not independent) outcomes for budgetary players. An extended discussion of the empirical justification for such a viewpoint and possible methods of model construction is found in Likens (1979).

How can competition for limited resources be dynamically modeled? What are the deductive consequences of such a model?

Competitive Models of Budgetary Interaction

From a purely logical point of view, a model that expresses change in an agency's or program's share of the budget should be able to produce at least four distinct qualitative behaviors, dependent on the particular substantive political conditions described by different parameters and initial conditions. These distinct qualitative behaviors rest on the assumption that economic conditions are more or less constant. In particular, we assume that no radical changes in tax structure occur and that no economic miracles or fabulous and unexpected increases in real economic productivity are feasible. (But this, of course, depends on the metric of measurement and some side economic hypotheses. After all, John Stuart Mill's steady-state economy is only literary up to this point in history.)

First, since resources are limited, one qualitative behavior should be growth in an agency's *share* of the budget to some upper limit. The classic incrementalist literature takes, as observed data, budget dollar amounts measured in current dollars. Taking a share of the budget as a measure of agency success provides a sharply different focus. Clearly, raw current dollar amounts can grow over time with no change in the delivery of real public goods and services if the inflation rate happens to match the incremental rate of agency budgetary growth. Equally, even if *real* growth occurs, the growth may be either generalized governmental growth or within budget competitive growth, i.e., shifts from one agency to another. These possibilities can only be considered through an analysis of budgetary *shares* or shares of some other meaningful economic aggregate such as gross national product. Hence, to recapitulate, an agency's *share* of the budget has some natural upper limit given scarce resources.

Second, since success is not always guaranteed over time, the model should also be able to eliminate altogether some unsuccessful agencies or programs from the budget. Third, since success for some agencies is virtually guaranteed (national defense and Congressmen's salaries, for example, will always secure a share of the budget), the model should be able to guarantee a lower limit on some agencies' shares of the budget total. And fourth, it seems likely that many agencies, *in the long run*, will acquire neither their minimal nor their maximal share of the budget, but will tend to attain something in between these two extremes. An acceptable model should, therefore, be able to predict change over time that, in the long run, converges on some equilibrium between the agency's lower and upper bounds. These qualitative behaviors are the most important a priori substantive requirement we impose on the modeling effort.

Further, it seems quite likely that the ultimate success or failure of a program or agency will in part depend on its current level of funding. That is, a program that is severely pinched for funds will find it difficult to provide services for its (shrinking) clientele; as political support diminishes, the chance for budgetary gains diminishes as well (Fenno, 1966). In contrast, an agency that is doing quite will in the budget process can provide useful services, expanding its base of political support and maintaining its aggressive budgetary posture. This implies, then, that there are *multiple equilibria* toward which an agency's share of the budget will move over time, depending (in part) upon its current share of the budget.

It is useful to note that *no* linear formalization can adequately represent the logic of this process. Since linear systems can at most exhibit a single

68

equilibrium point, a nonlinear representation with the possibility of multiple equilibria is logically required. Regardless of the particular incremental or nonincremental assumptions of the model, the substantive properties of the budgetary phenomenon logically require a nonlinear dynamic formalization.

The Logic of Competition

In order to examine the consequences of *competitive interdependence* among agencies, two nonlinear models are developed in several steps. First, consider a single agency and denote its budget share by X_t. We wish to characterize the changes in the quantity X_t in a way that specifies the dependence of those changes on the appropriations for a second agency, Y_t. Hence write

$$\Delta X_t = f[X_t, Y_t, U_t] \qquad [5.3]$$

Interpret equation 5.3 as asserting that changes in the success of agency X depend on the agency's past level of success in the competition, X_t; how well other agencies (in particular the principle competitor Y) have been doing, Y_t; and current economic and political conditions that may influence relative success rates, denoted by U_t. We assume that these exogenous inputs, U_t, enter the process in a linearly additive fashion. Hence, rewrite equation 5.3 as

$$\Delta X_t = f[X_t, Y_t] + g[U_t]. \qquad [5.4]$$

An analogous argument for agency Y obtains. To keep matters tractable we restrict our attention to this bilateral case of two-agency competition only. However, it is important to realize that a generalization to multiple-agency competitions is straightforward and follows naturally along the lines of the present development.

The presence of current levels of agency success, X_t and Y_t, as arguments of the function f represents, formally and technically, the substantive motivation of our development—agencies are interdependent in the budgetary process.

A number of formulations can be constructed to obtain a representation of the system of joint competition. We follow an operator notation strategy. Define a_t and b_t as variable rates of change operating on the fortunes of agencies X and Y, respectively. These operators will be assumed to function *proportionally* to the current levels of success for the agencies, measured by X_t and Y_t, and also to be *functions of* those same current levels of success, X_t and Y_t. These assumptions are now sufficient to allow us to write a system of equations for the competition between agencies X and Y as

$$\Delta X_t = a_t X_t + U_t \qquad\qquad [5.5]$$

$$\Delta Y_t = b_t Y_t + U_t \qquad\qquad [5.6]$$

where the state variables, X_t and Y_t, denote *shares* of the budget (total, total controllable, total functional, and so forth), acquired by programs or agencies X and Y at time t; U_t denotes exogenous inputs; a_t and b_t are variable rates of change for X_t and Y_t, such that a_t and b_t are both functions of X_t and Y_t.

Making a_t and b_t depend on the levels of success X_t and Y_t, coupled with the explicit functional form assumption specified in equations 5.5 and 5.6, means that the model to be exhibited will be inherently non-linear. This is true not because a substantive and formal interdependence has been specified between agencies X and Y, but because the formalizations of equations 5.5 and 5.6 logically entail nonlinearity given our substantive hypotheses on a_t and b_t, namely, that they also depend on the current levels of the states X and Y. (In the Richardson arms' race model interdependence between states is achieved while simultaneously preserving linearity. The present development follows a different strategy.)

Obviously, it is often the case that more than two agencies or programs are in simultaneous competition for resources. Here, however, the emphasis will be on the simpler and more easily understood case of only two competitors. While some realism may be lost, the practice of studying reduced systems is scientifically sound (Hirsch and Smale, 1974: 75).

Further, to incorporate the central theme of competition between agencies and programs, both models include the qualitative assumption that *an increase in the magnitude of the budget of one agency decreases the rate of budgetary growth of its competitor (or increases its rate of decay)*. That is,

$$\partial a_t / \partial Y_t < 0 \qquad\qquad [5.7]$$

and

$$\partial b_t / \partial X_t < 0 \qquad\qquad [5.8]$$

Finally, since we are working with budget shares, each model incorporates the assumption that there are levels of funding (in shares) toward which X_t and Y_t will naturally tend *in the absence of* competition and exogenous inputs. Denote these natural limits for X and Y as L_x and L_y, respectively, and assume them to be constant for significant historical epochs. This assumption may then generally be expressed as:

$$a_t > 0 \quad \text{for} \quad X_t < L_x \qquad\qquad [5.9]$$

$$a_t < 0 \quad \text{for} \quad X_t > L_x \qquad\qquad [5.10]$$

$$a_t = 0 \quad \text{for} \quad X_t = L_x \qquad\qquad [5.11]$$

and

$$b_t > 0 \quad \text{for} \quad Y_t < L_y \qquad\qquad [5.12]$$

$$b_t < 0 \quad \text{for} \quad Y_t > L_y \qquad\qquad [5.13]$$

$$b_t = 0 \quad \text{for} \quad Y_t = L_y \qquad\qquad [5.14]$$

Expressions 5.9 through 5.14 are abstract and formal, but their substantive interpretations should be made clear. For example, expression 5.10 articulates the condition that whenever the current level of budget support for agency X exceeds its natural limit, the sign of the growth operator a_t should be strictly negative, producing negative change and thus moving the state level X_t down toward its natural level, L_x, given that exogenous inputs have been disregarded and budgetary outcomes are (temporarily assumed) independent for all players.

There are, of course, numerous formalizations that could incorporate these basic assumptions. Two models are studied here. The first is a model of "pure" competition in which the intensity of interaction between competitors is largely unrestricted. The second is a more realistic representation, where a degree of structural protection exists for each competitor against encroachment by others.

The notion of structural protection is aimed at capturing the idea that some agencies are favored, at least for minimum levels of program effort, by the long-run structure of social, economic, and hence general political conditions. Thus, the principal variant of the pure competition model is one in which a long-run bias operates in the system, protecting some minimal base for each competitor.

Model I: Unrestrained Budgetary Competition

To achieve a model of unrestrained competition between two interacting agencies or programs that captures our central notions, we make an explicit assumption for a_t in equation 5.5. Furthermore, to avoid substantively important but technically trivial difficulties, we set $U_t = 0$. Hence, write

$$a_t = p_x(L_x - X_t) - c_y Y_t \qquad\qquad [5.15]$$

In keeping with our earlier arguments, this substitution for the operator a_t depends on the limit, L_x; the current level of success of agency X, X_t, and the current level of success of its principal competitor Y, Y_t; and it introduces two new terms in the form of parameters, p_x and c_y, all gathered together in an explicit functional form. When equation 5.15 and the hypothesis of zero exogenous inputs are applied to equation 5.5 we may write

$$\Delta X_t = [p_x(L_x - X_t) - c_y Y_t]X_t \qquad [5.16]$$

Equation 5.16 can be read as asserting that change in the level of budgetary success of agency X, ΔX_t, is proportional at a characteristic rate p_x to the difference between natural agency limit, L_x, and its current level, X_t, combined with a discounting factor arising from competition with agency Y, operating proportionally to the current level of success, X_t. This discounting factor operates proportionally to both current agency success, X_t, and current competitor success, Y_t, at a characteristic rate c_y. The minus sign that occurs in equation 5.16 simply indicates the substantive notion that competition is at least partially zero-sum—what agency Y receives comes partially out of the hide of agency X. An analogous argument holds for agency Y. We assume competition is symmetric, and thus are justified in writing

$$\Delta Y_t = [p_y(L_y - Y_t) - c_x X_t]Y_t \qquad [5.17]$$

To review, the state variables X_t and Y_t are proportions of some relevant budget total received by programs or agencies X and Y. The parameters L_x and L_y denote the maximal share of the total budget that the agency would receive in the absence of competition, assuming zero exogenous inputs. These upper limits (L_x and L_y) are assumed to be constant for significant historical periods and are determined by the broad policy objectives extant during the era, the general ability of competitors, administrators' political skills, and similar factors.

The parameters p_x and p_y denote the general objective success of X and Y, respectively, as budgetary players. The larger p_x or p_y, the greater is that agency's average net objective performance in securing its optimal funding level, L_x or L_y.

Notice that, as the model is written, the greater the agency's average success, p_i, the more rapidly it will tend to approach some optimal share of the budget. This assumption has been suggested in at least two empirical studies (Sharkansky, 1965, 1968). In this context, an agency or program is likely to have greater success as a budgetary competitor if it is headed by people who are highly motivated and articulate political entrepreneurs with experience in bureaucratic infighting. Alternatively, a newly established agency or program with relatively unskilled or inexperienced leadership would tend to have a lower level of effectiveness as a budgetary player for some significant historical period.

Whether experience, motivation, and/or aggressiveness is the deciding factor is beyond the scope of the model and certainly beyond most readily available observations. The parameters p_x and p_y capture a net objective result of an obviously complex process. Thus, in this instance the necessary simplification of reality is especially stark, but without this simplification the modeling task could not proceed. Such simplification is justified if it yields sufficient insight into the logic underlying the process.

Finally, the parameter c_y denotes the rate at which Y competes against X, and c_x denotes the rate of competition by X against Y. These parameters provide a measure of how significantly or successfully each agency encroaches on the other's funds.

The logic of the model is straightforward. It asserts that, *in the absence of competition* ($c_y = c_x = 0$), X_t and Y_t approach their upper limits (L_x and L_y) according to the logistic law (see Chapter 3) for each player, i.e., independently:

$$\Delta X_t = p_x(L_x - X_t)X_t \tag{5.18}$$

$$\Delta Y_t = p_y(L_y - Y_t)Y_t \tag{5.19}$$

Assuming, of course, that $0 < p_y, p_x < 1$, equations 5.18 and 5.19 produce the familiar S-curve typical of diffusion processes (see Chapter 3). Note, however, that if p_x and p_y are unrestricted, the system may be overdriven and smooth behavior may disappear.

For competitive processes, c_x and c_y are assumed to lie between zero and unity, and hence the larger either agency becomes, the greater becomes its competitive impact on the other. There is nothing in the structure of the process that limits how much the agencies can influence each other. In this sense, then, the competition may be characterized as "pure" or "unrestrained."

EQUILIBRIA IN PURE COMPETITION

Equilibria for the system are obtained as always, by setting $\Delta Y_t = \Delta X_t = 0$:

$$0 = [p_x(L_x - X^*) - c_y Y^*]X^* \tag{5.20}$$

$$0 = [p_y(L_y - Y^*) - c_x X^*]Y^* \tag{5.21}$$

There are four simultaneous solutions for (X^*, Y^*):

$$(X^*, Y^*) = (0,0) \tag{5.22}$$

$$(X^*, Y^*) = (0, L_y) \tag{5.23}$$

$$(X^*, Y^*) = (L_x, 0) \tag{5.24}$$

$$(X^*, Y^*) = ([p_y p_x L_x - c_y L_y]/[p_y p_x - c_y c_x], \tag{5.25}$$
$$[p_x p_y L_y - c_x L_x]/[p_x p_y - c_y c_x])$$

Net change ceases, then, under four conditions:

(1) when both agencies are eliminated,
(2) when agency X is eliminated and agency Y obtains its upper limit, Ly,
(3) when agency Y is eliminated and X achieves its optimal level, L_x, and
(4) when both achieve some competitive level between zero and their upper limits.

Given that three of the four possibilities end in elimination of one or both agencies, it is clear that unrestrained budgetary competition is quite Darwinian. In addition, this unlimited competition—with its rather extreme consequences—is unrealistic in the context of contemporary federal budgeting. Agencies and programs in the real world are seldom totally eliminated. At worst they tend to move to some minimal level of funding that they then maintain year after year.

This model might well describe budgetary competition in political settings that are not highly bureaucratized. It may describe, for example, programmatic conflict in newly initiated agencies where priorities are not well established and bureaucratic inertia has not yet mounted.

PHASE-SPACE REPRESENTATION OF THE NONLINEAR SYSTEM

Unlike the nonlinear model of Chapter 3, this nonlinear system possesses no closed-form solution. Thus, our choice of analytic strategies is more circumscribed. The qualitative behavior of the model is most easily studied in the *phase space*. That is, rather than examining the behavior of X_t and Y_t each as a function of time, examine Y_t as a function of X_t (or vice versa) through time, i.e., eliminate explicit representation of time. (As outlined in Chapter 4 this is the geometric strategy for studying autonomous systems.)

A state-space or phase-space representation projects the three-dimensional graph of X_t, Y_t, and t onto the two-dimensional $[X_t, Y_t]$ plane. Such a projection in graphic form is usually termed a "phase portrait." The principal question is: Under what substantive conditions are the different equilibria reached? What is the likelihood that one or both agencies may be eliminated, or that both agencies survive over time? Qualitatively, the phase portrait exhibits a picture of these dynamics that emphasizes the substantive competition of the two agencies sequenced in *any arbitrary, discrete-time* metric.

The projections may be displayed as graphs, which are compared for different parameter value assumptions. Thus, as parameter values vary the qualitative differences in system behavior may be easily (and vividly) exhibited in the state space (X,Y). Begin by setting equations 5.16 and 5.17 equal to zero and obtaining one nonzero point locus for $\Delta X_t = 0$ and one for $\Delta Y_1 = 0$. These nontrivial loci are

$$Y_t = [p_x/c_y]X_t + [p_x/c_y]L_x \qquad \text{(for } \Delta X_t = 0) \qquad [5.26]$$

and

$$Y_t = [-c_x/p_y]X_t + L_y \qquad \text{(for } \Delta Y_t = 0) \qquad [5.27]$$

For this particular nonlinear model it is possible to obtain explicit representations of these zero-change conditions for Y as a function of X. The fact that these loci form two straight lines is just well-planned good luck; there is no guarantee that more complex nonlinear models will always be so obliging. If the model proves intractable at this point, a local stability analysis is probably all that is possible.

For our purposes we disregard the zero loci formed by the X and Y axes and focus on those given by equations 5.26 and 5.27. By construction, when X_t is on its zero-change locus, the change in X_t equals zero; and when Y_t is on its zero-change locus, the change of Y_t equals zero. One implication, then, is that whenever and wherever these curves intersect, that intersection is an equilibrium point for the system, since $\Delta X_t = \Delta Y_t = 0$.

The question, then, is what happens when X_t and Y_t move off these zero-change loci? Using graph techniques, it is easily determined for this model that, whenever X_t is to the right of its zero-change line, ΔX_t is negative. We can also determine the behavior of ΔX_t when X_t is to the left of its zero-change line. Thus, in the first quadrant, at any point to the right of the $\Delta X_t = 0$ locus, ΔX_t is negative; to the left, ΔX_t is positive. A similar analysis may be performed for the ΔY_t zero-change line, and the reader might like to verify that above the $\Delta Y_t = 0$ line ΔY_t is negative and below it ΔY_t is positive.[11]

If we then know where (X_t, Y_t) is with respect to the zero-change lines, we can immediately determine the direction of (X_t, Y_t) at time $(t + 1)$. In effect, each of the zero-change loci "pull" the point (X_t, Y_t) toward themselves, with Y_t able to move only up and down, X_t only able to move left and right, and with the pull proportional to the magnitude of the displacement. (A very similar geometric interpretation was originally used by Richardson in analyzing his arms race model). Combining the two motions gives the vector traveled by (X_t, Y_t) from t to $(t + 1)$. For example, if the point (X_t, Y_t) is above the $\Delta Y_t = 0$ locus and to the left of the $\Delta X_t = 0$ locus, (X_t, Y_t) will move down and to the right from t to $(t + 1)$. The reader may wish to compare this to the construction in Chapter 4.

The $\Delta X_t = 0$ and $\Delta Y_t = 0$ loci produce six distinct geometries in the phase space. Three geometries occur when the slope of the $\Delta X_t = 0$ line is greater than the slope of the $\Delta Y_t = 0$ line. Three different geometries exist when the magnitude of the slopes is reversed. The six possibilities are exhibited in Figure 5.1, and for each possibility the qualitative behavior of (X_t, Y_t) is displayed. Inspection of Figure 5.1 provides a global analysis of the system's dynamics for the first quadrant (the only state space with substantive meaning for this model.)

Algebraic formulations that yield direct substantive interpretations can be constructed for a number of these geometries. Recall that p_x gives the average success or skill of X and that L_x is a measure of the maximal

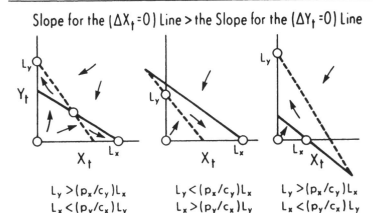

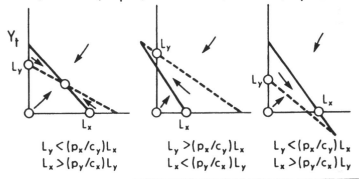

Figure 5.1 Geometries of the Zero-Change Loci

position of X with respect to all other relevant competitors. Thus, the term (p_xL_x) may be conceptualized as the net objective success of X as a budgetary player. In simple terms, (p_xL_x) measures the agency's budgetary clout. Since the parameter c_x expresses the impact of X on Y, the term c_xL_x may be interpreted as the net competitive impact of X on the budgetary success of Y. Similar interpretations hold for the terms p_yL_y and c_yL_y. These expressions may be used to characterize various conditions in the first quadrant, yielding the following set of substantive conclusions:

(1) Agency X eliminates Y if (a) the net objective success of X exceeds the competitive impact of agency Y $(p_xL_x > c_yL_y)$, and (b) the net objective success of Y is insufficient to defend adequately against

76

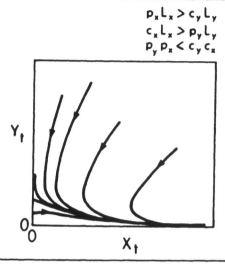

$$p_x L_x > c_y L_y$$
$$c_x L_x > p_y L_y$$
$$p_y p_x < c_y c_x$$

Figure 5.2 X Eliminates Y

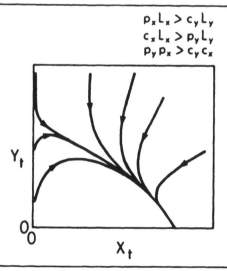

$$p_x L_x > c_y L_y$$
$$c_x L_x > p_y L_y$$
$$p_y p_x > c_y c_x$$

Figure 5.3 X Eliminates Y

competition by X ($c_x L_x > p_y L_y$). Typical phase portraits are exhibited in Figures 5.2 and 5.3.

(2) Agency Y eliminates X if the above inequalities are reversed. That is, the success of Y overcomes the competitive impact of X, while X lacks sufficient clout to defend itself adequately against

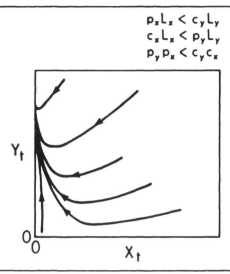

$$p_x L_x < c_y L_y$$
$$c_x L_x < p_y L_y$$
$$p_y p_x < c_y c_x$$

Y_t

X_t

Figure 5.4   Y Eliminates X

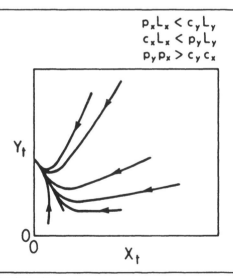

$$p_x L_x < c_y L_y$$
$$c_x L_x < p_y L_y$$
$$p_y p_x > c_y c_x$$

Y_t

X_t

Figure 5.5   Y Eliminates X

encroachment by Y. Phase portraits resulting from this set of political conditions are exhibited in Figures 5.4 and 5.5.

(3) Agencies X and Y both survive if both are strong enough to defend themselves adequately against encroachment by the other, and if the effects of competition are not so great as to destabilize the agencies' interaction ($p_y p_x > c_y c_x$). Figure 5.6 provides a typical

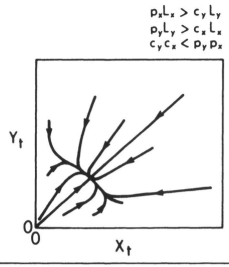

$$p_x L_x > c_y L_y$$
$$p_y L_y > c_x L_x$$
$$c_y c_x < p_y p_x$$

Figure 5.6 Destabilizing Competition and Mutual Coexistence

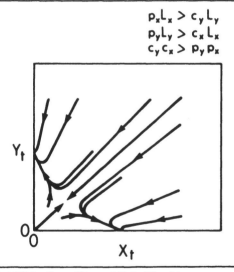

$$p_x L_x > c_y L_y$$
$$p_y L_y > c_x L_x$$
$$c_y c_x > p_y p_x$$

Figure 5.7 Destabilizing Competition and Mutual Coexistence

phase portrait of the situation in which the agencies manage mutual coexistence. When competition becomes sufficiently intense, however, it tends to destabilize even this situation and the result is the elimination of one agency or the other. As Figure 5.7 illustrates, initial conditions determine the ultimate success, with the relatively stronger agency at time $t = 0$ finally prevailing.

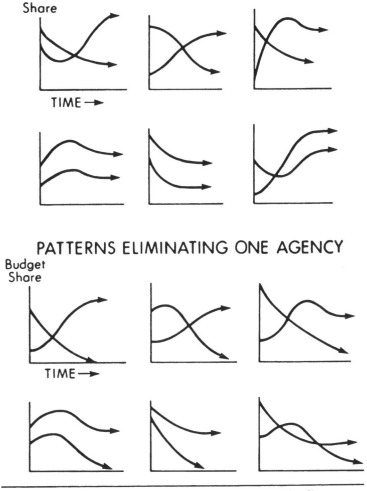

Figure 5.8 Histories of Appropriations for Competing Agencies as Budget Shares

It is apparent from these phase portraits of the model that a variety of histories may be generated for the competing agencies. While all of the possible time series cannot be represented here, it is instructive to present several of the more common interaction patterns predicted by the model. Figure 5.8 exhibits several typical deterministic histories that are generated by this nonlinear dynamic structure.

Model II: Restricted Competition

Constraints may be imposed on the interaction described by the preceding model in a number of ways. We confine our discussion to a single elementary modeling strategy—placing lower bounds on X_t and Y_t, such that spending below these minimal levels is highly improbable.

Denoting these levels as B_x and B_y, these lower limits may be incorporated in the preceding model by writing

$$\Delta X_t = [p_x(L_x - X_t) - c_y Y_t]X_t[X_t - B_x] \qquad [5.28]$$

$$\Delta Y_t = [p_y(L_y - Y_t) - c_x X_t]Y_t[Y_t - B_y] \qquad [5.29]$$

The central logic of competitive interdependence remains unchanged. The important difference is that the interaction of X and Y now occurs in a structurally limited context. For example, if X is losing ground—moving closer to its lower bound—the term $(X_t - B_x)$ gets smaller and smaller: The effect of further interaction is increasingly reduced. And as Y approaches its lower bound, B_y, the impact of X on Y is increasingly minimized. This is a modeling device that is frequently useful and worth noting.

Forcing this constraint on the interaction of X and Y has the technical effect of moving the dynamics from a coupled quadratic system to a cubic one. The substantive consequences are striking. The most obvious change is the multiplicity of outcomes that is now possible. The reader should convince himself or herself that not only are the four equilibria of the preceding model possible, but *five additional equilibria* now exist. While we do not exhibit these equilibria, their interpretation follows a now familiar logic. The system stabilizes when both competitors are eliminated, when both are at their lower limits, when one is eliminated and the other is either at its minimal level or its maximal level, when one is at its minimal level while the other obtains more than its minimum but less than its maximum, and when both maintain levels that lie between their lower and upper bounds.

A graph analysis of this dynamic system proceeds exactly as before. Six unique geometries exist, but the addition of the zero-change loci $Y_t = B_y$ (for $\Delta Y_t = 0$) and $X_t = B_x$ (for $\Delta X_t = 0$) produce somewhat more complex behaviors. The interested reader should consult Likens (1979).

It is easily shown that under normal initial conditions (i.e., $B_x < X_t < L_x$ and $B_y < Y_t < L_y$) the competitors are guaranteed at least a minimal share of resources. In the less usual circumstance that one competitor is initially below its minimal level, or is abruptly pushed below it by short-term political forces, the results are more problematic. It is sometimes possible for the competitor to recover, or the competitor may be altogether eliminated. If both players are initially funded below their minima, both are always eliminated.

The model, then, can generate all of the qualitative behaviors that are logically required of a model of budgetary competition. Placing limitations on "pure" competitive processes generates dynamics that seem both logically and politically realistic. To summarize, the model provides for growth in an agency's share of the budget to some upper limit, allows for the elimination of unsuccessful agencies from the budget, guarantees a lower limit on some agencies' shares of the budget total, and predicts change over time that, in the long run, converges on some equilibrium between an agency's lower and upper bounds.

Conclusion

The models presented in this chapter attempt to express the dynamics of resource allocation as inherently competitive, and often conflictive, in nature. It is worth emphasizing that while the analysis does not depend critically on the presence of only two competitors, increasing the number of players is not without consequence.

From a technical perspective, increasing the number of states in a system, particularly if the system is nonlinear, makes it increasingly difficult to obtain a global analysis of the system. With only two states, graph-analytic techniques may be quite instructive. With three states, graphics are three-dimensional and tricky at best. With four or more states, graph-analytic techniques break down altogether, and a local stability analysis must suffice.

From a substantive perspective, increasing the number of competitors will produce an increasingly rich political fabric in which a tremendously varied dynamic landscape may occur. In the sense of LaPorte (1975) or Brunner and Brewer (1971), increasing the number of competitors (and hence the level of interdependence in the process) naturally increases the probability of generating unanticipated consequences that may or may not be socially or politically optimal, and these may be generated by only small perturbations of system states, or small alterations in parameter values.

6. DYNAMIC MODELING AS A SCIENTIFIC ENTERPRISE

Dynamic modeling in the social sciences proceeds at many levels of abstraction, in widely differing substantive contexts. The basic request the investigator makes of *any* model in *any* context is this: Does the model do the scientific work required of it? Put another way, does the model adequately respond to the problem that motivated its development? A continuum of possible models ranges from detailed, data-oriented, complex, descriptive models aimed at practical use to abstract, theoretical, non-data-oriented, simplified, only crudely descriptive models aimed at providing general insight (May, 1974). We have worked on the side of theoretical models, but they are not purely abstract for we have kept empirical interpretations continually in focus.

The question then emerges: Is this a useful and reasonable strategy? To their credit, simple models provide a measure of manageability. For example, the mathematical theory for linear forms is complete, equilibria are global, and stability may be completely and globally analyzed. More complex models are more realistic and capture the details of the process, but quickly become unmanageable. These are choices that provide differing bargains under differing conditions. It is not *better* to do theoretical modeling rather than more empirically oriented descriptive statistical modeling. Nor is it *better* to do the latter. The models we offer clearly possess empirical content with relatively straightforward, substantive interpretations. They are, however, far removed from the pole of detailed, complex, descriptive models; and from the opposite pole of more abstract, theorem-proving, pure mathematical models (Ferejohn and Noll, 1978). Thus, the present offering occupies an empirical and theoretical middle ground.

An Overview of Model Structure

The reader may find it useful to review the logical forms of the models we have developed in this monograph, their common substantive interpretations, and the principal differences among them in terms of qualitative behaviors. The first model of mobilization was a first-order linear difference equation with constant coefficients. It may be characterized as the time series of a single state variable, in this case voting data, and uses only that single observable (and its lag) in model construction and estimation. Since the model is linear the solution form is known, the equilibrium point can be determined, and its stability can be evaluated globally. And, even though the model is linear, it potentially exhibits four different curvilinear behaviors in the time domain: monotonic convergence to a limit, oscillatory convergence to a limit, monotonic divergence, and oscillatory divergence.

The second model is a first-order nonlinear (quadratic) difference equation with constant coefficients. Again, the model uses a time series of a single state variable, such as voting data, but in this instance we employ the variable, its lag, and the square of its lag. Social interaction is built into the model by making a random mixing assumption, and other similar nonlinear models have been used to study social interaction processes in voting (Kohfeld, 1979) and mass compliance (Likens and Kohfeld, 1980; Kohfeld and Likens, 1982). In general, the theory for nonlinear models is incomplete, solution forms are not usually available, equilibria are multiple, and only local stability can be analyzed. The quadratic is a special form, however, and results that can be applied to determine global stability are available (Chaundy and Phillips, 1936). Nonlinear models produce an especially rich variety of time paths: the logistic growth curve, extended period oscillation, and other more complicated patterns.

The third model is a system of first-order linear equations that also can be written as a single, higher-order linear difference equation. Since the higher-order equation is linear, the underlying mathematical theory is complete. Systems of first-order linear equations can be used to represent complex patterns of interdependence, and a number of strategies are available for exploiting their potential: matrix representations of system structure, phase space interpretations of a system's qualitative behavior, and stability analyses using the system solution. Higher-order models are also useful to an analysis of the substantive and technical consequences of time delay in feedback mechanisms.

The final model presented is a system of nonlinear equations. The most interesting feature of the nonlinear system construction is the structure of reasoning employed to arrive at the final model forms. First, the substantive literature (budgeting) was briefly covered. Second, the minimum qualitative properties of a reasonable formal model solution were developed. Third, a strategy of modeling was employed that, at every step, built on these a priori requirements in developing the model *form*. And finally, general mathematical theory was invoked to investigate the properties of the model, and to show that the model possessed the desired properties; i.e., the model met the problems that motivated its development. In the case of this nonlinear system, the phase-plane interpretation of qualitative behavior once again emerges as an important analytic device.

These models share several important features: structural parameters that are constant in time, dynamic properties that logically flow from model construction, and, for two of the models, multiple but interdependent system states. We consider these features before summarizing the steps in model development.

Multiple and Interdependent System States

An important structural feature of the latter two models, and a particularly important feature of any multiple-state model, is the concept of *interdependence*. Interdependence means that change in one state of a social system depends on (and produces) change in other states of the system. This is equivalent to the statement that *many elements of social reality are dynamically interrelated*. Change in one social phenomenon often has the effect of a pebble tossed into a quiet pond: It is likely to ripple through many other interrelated activities and phenomena.

While the specific interdependent structures vary across different models, the patterns of interaction are *always limited to six distinct qualitative types*. These different patterns of interdependence may be represented in a qualitative sign matrix (see May, 1974; Kohfeld, 1976; Likens, 1978) with elements that are (+) for positive change resulting from interaction, (-) for negative interaction effects, and (0) for no effect.

		Effect of State j on i		
		+	−	0
Effect	+	(+,+)	(+,−)	(+,0)
of State	−	(−,+)	(−,−)	(−,0)
i on j	0	(0,+)	(0,−)	(0,0)

In biological terms, (0,0) signifies no interaction, (0,+) signifies amensalism, (0,−) is parasitism, (+,+) is symbiosis, (+,−) is predation, and (−,−) is competition. Social science analogs are readily identified: The dynamics of the Richardson arms race model, for example, is analogous to a symbiotic system, and interagency battles for budgetary resources are best described as a competitive dynamic system.

Social dynamics are often interdependent dynamics. Change is not isolated; it is interactive. The dynamic interactions that can occur are limited to a very manageable set of qualitative patterns, and all of these patterns are potentially observed within various social activities and processes.

Structural Parameters

The models' structural parameters control dynamic behavior, and they share several features. First, the system parameters are always assumed to be *fixed* for finite periods of time. The time dependence of the processes is not reflected in the parameters; they are temporally independent during periods for which the process is synchronic.

Second, the models' parameters are of two different logical types. Many of the parameters express *rates of change for different components of the model*. These are typically interpreted in the applications as gain or loss rates, rates of mobilization, rates of aggressiveness, rates of success, and so forth. In addition, several formalizations include one or more parameters that express *naturally occurring limits or natural levels for certain states of the system*. These parameters often arise as the result of formal or informal institutional arrangements within the structure of the process. An upper limit on political mobilization was hypothesized as the result of political socialization and the institutional norms it produces. A lower bound for agency appropriations was hypothesized as one of many institutional arrangements designed to reduce conflict within the budgetary process. In each case system change is at least partially controlled by those temporally fixed parameters that express *rates* and those that express naturally occurring *limits*—maxima, minima, or endpoints.

System Properties

Once an acceptable formalization of the system structure is developed, certain of its logical properties become quite important. These properties generally concern how and where the process moves across time. More precisely, a dynamic formalization of the process leads to questions regarding equilibria, stability, and the descriptive qualities of time paths.

In focusing on *equilibria* the investigator is concerned with system states that remain numerically constant across time. It should be re-emphasized that even when the net change of the system states is zero, a tremendous amount of change can be occurring within the process. People still change their opinions, agencies still compete for dollars, and so forth. The numerical values of the system states remain constant because all change is balanced, not because change is absent. If the system states approach their equilibrium values over time, the process may be characterized as exhibiting *stability*. A more rigorous definition is that a stable process will return toward equilibrium when its states are perturbed; an unstable process will not.

Combining information about system equilibria and stability, the investigator may then develop a strong sense of the system's *qualitative behavior*, the particular history of outputs that a model generates across time. Here the focus is on the particular features of the history, revealed graphically through a *time path* of the states of the system for different parameters and initial conditions. Alternatively, insights about the qualitative behavior of the process may be gained through examination of a *phase portrait*, the simultaneous trajectories of the states across time with respect to each other, with time suppressed as an explicit quantity.

A number of questions emerge regarding the dynamics exhibited by a process. Will the process asymptotically approach some limiting value over time? Under what conditions will the process oscillate, with what periodicity? Can the process reproduce certain patterns—growth and then decay to a limit, for example? How, in short, will the states move across time, and what central tendencies should be empirically observed?

Steps in Model Development

In summary, the two key components in each of the substantive chapters are the formalization and its mathematical analysis. An examination of the formalizations and their analytics underscores the importance of two separate steps in any modeling endeavor.

The first step begins with the implicit question: "Of what is reality composed?" As Quine (1961) informs us, there is universal agreement that reality is composed of everything; disagreement is over special cases. More precisely, then, the modeling task begins with the construction of a still life portrait—the abstract characterization of a social process at a point in time. In each formalization the social process is conceived in such a manner as to reduce a set of complex verbal intuitions to a more manageable set of observable (or unobservable) system states.

Once an acceptable static characterization is in hand, formalization proceeds by asking a second question: What are the laws of change? How is reality transformed by the logic of the process with which we are concerned? This second step forces the investigator to make explicit statements and assumptions regarding the structure of temporal interdependence. The rigor of difference equations, coupled with the analytic potential they provide, allows an examination of the consequences that flow from these laws of change. In this way we move closer to our goal: an understanding of the logic underlying social process and social change.

APPENDIX

Difference Equation Forms

Difference equations can be algebraically manipulated to produce a number of different forms. Three such equation forms are basic and are illustrated below. Consider the following difference equation model:

$$\Delta Y_t = a_0 - a_1 Y_{t-1} \qquad [A.1]$$

This model is in a *recursive* form when an isolated left-hand side system state is defined in terms of its own lagged values and constants:

$$Y_{t+1} = a_0 + (1 - a_1) Y_t \qquad [A.2]$$

The model is in a *canonical* form when all system states are on the left-hand side, and all constants are on the right-hand side:

$$Y_{t+1} - (1 - a_1) Y_t = a_0 \qquad [A.3]$$

Finally, the model is in a *homogeneous* form if the left-hand side system states are set equal to zero:

$$Y_{t+1} - (1 - a_1) Y_t = 0 \qquad [A.4]$$

Matrix Manipulations of the Arms Race Model

It is often useful to solve systems of dynamic equations using Cramer's rule. Solution by Cramer's rule calls for forming the ratio of two determinants. The denominator of the ratio is the determinant of the coefficient matrix, and the numerator is the determinant of the matrix of coefficients after the right-hand side vector has been substituted for the column of coefficients whose sequence number from left to right corresponds to the system state sequence number from top to bottom.

Applying this rule, the system in equation 4.11 may be solved as follows:

$$X_t = \frac{\det \begin{pmatrix} g & -k \\ g' & (\Delta + a') \end{pmatrix}}{\det \begin{pmatrix} (\Delta + a) & -k \\ -k' & (\Delta + a') \end{pmatrix}} \qquad [A.5]$$

$$Y_t = \frac{\det \begin{pmatrix} (\Delta + a) & g \\ -k' & g' \end{pmatrix}}{\det \begin{pmatrix} (\Delta + a) & -k \\ -k' & (\Delta + a') \end{pmatrix}} \qquad [A.6]$$

Computing the determinants for X_t and Y_t we obtain

$$X_t = \frac{\Delta g + ga' + kg'}{\Delta^2 + (a + a')\Delta + aa' - kk'} \qquad [A.7]$$

$$Y_t = \frac{\Delta g' + g'a + k'g}{\Delta^2 + (a + a')\Delta + aa' - kk'} \qquad [A.8]$$

Now treat the left-hand sides as ratios (X_t and Y_t are implicitly divided by one), and cross-multiply obtaining

$$[\Delta^2 + (a + a')\Delta + aa' - kk']X_t = \Delta g + ga' + kg' \qquad [A.9]$$

$$[\Delta^2 + (a + a')\Delta + aa' - kk']Y_t = \Delta g' + g'a + k'g \qquad [A.10]$$

The terms involving delta on the right-hand side drop out since the first difference of a constant is zero, leaving only well-defined constants whose values are known, at least in principle. These are the system inputs or forcing functions and they need not be constant but may be known functions of time, or, in empirical applications may be observables.

The left-hand sides of equations A.9 and A.10 can be thought of as specifying a rule for operating on the system states X_t and Y_t. The first term, Δ^2, says take a first difference of the state twice. The second term, $(a + a')\Delta$, directs us to take a first difference and then multiply by the sum of two constants. The third and fourth terms, aa' and $-kk'$, simply indicate multiplication by constants. The reader might like to make those calculations and compare them with the results

$$X_{t+2} + (2 - a - a')X_{t+1} + (1 + aa' - kk' - a - a')X_t = ga' + kg' \quad [A.11]$$

$$Y_{t+2} + (a + a' - 2)Y_{t+1} + (1 + aa' - kk' - a - a')Y_t = g'a + k'g \quad [A.12]$$

Equations A.11 and A.12 are *canonical* forms used below in obtaining a closed-form solution for the system specified in equations 4.9 and 4.10.

Finally, rewrite equations A.11 and A.12 as

$$X_{t+2} = (2 - a - a)X_{t+1} + (a + a' + kk' - aa' - 1)X_t + ga' + kg' \quad [A.13]$$

$$Y_{t+2} = (2 - a - a')Y_{t+1} + (a + a' + kk' - aa' - 1)Y_t + g'a + k'g \quad [A.14]$$

Equations A.13 and A.14 are identical with equations 4.7 and 4.8 obtained earlier by main force and artistry.

The approach by Cramer's rule is especially convenient for determining the equilibrium values for X_t and Y_t. When the original left-hand side deltas are all set to zero, all determinant terms involving delta disappear. This leads immediately, using equations A.7 and A.8 to

$$X^* = (ga' + g'k)/(aa' - kk') \qquad [A.15]$$

and

$$Y^* = (g'a + gk')/(aa' - kk') \qquad [A.16]$$

as the values of the equilibrium vector S^*.

Continuous versus Discrete Time Models

The similarities and distinctions between difference and differential equation models are best illustrated by considering the solutions and behavior patterns of these two types of equations. The analogies between the two should not be underemphasized. Existence and uniqueness theorems, theorems on qualitative behaviors, and even the solution forms themselves appear in highly analogous ways in the corresponding chapters of difference and differential equation texts. These mathematical similarities, however, should not obscure the fact that there are important differences between the two types of equations that are particularly relevant in applied work. In some instances solutions can be determined for a differential equation, but not for the analogous difference equation. Furthermore, even if both equations can be solved, the solutions may be quite different: In particular, the qualitative and the quantitative behavior of the two equations will be different under certain conditions. To illustrate these points we discuss the availability and nature of solutions for first- and second-order equations. These equations are chosen because social science applications seldom involve higher-order equations, and the extension from a second-order equation to equations of higher-order is generally straightforward.

The first-order linear differential equation is the simplest to consider, and can usually be solved by obtaining an integrating factor. Thus, assuming that the relevant integrals can be found in tables of integrals and using various techniques of integration, solutions for these equations are tractable for most applications. For the first-order linear difference equation general solutions depend upon finding inverse difference operators—a difficult task at best. Thus, aside from the special case in which the coefficients are constant, it may be very difficult to solve even the first-order linear difference equation.

For higher-order linear equations and for nonlinear equations, the advantages of differential equations that accrue as a result of calculus become less significant, although by no means unimportant. In general, the second-order linear differential equation can be solved if one solution of the homogeneous portion or a particular solution of the complete equation is known. Analogous information for the second-order linear difference equation renders the problem similar to that of finding solutions for the first-order equation (see Brand, 1966: chs. 3 and 8, for details). Thus, neither equation has a readily available soluton. However, if information about a portion of the solution is available, it will generally be easier to solve the differential equation.

This conclusion also applies to higher-order linear equations and to nonlinear equations. In these cases it is often very difficult to find solutions for either type of equation. There is no general method for solving even first-order nonlinear differential equations, and the fact that existence theorems abound is of dubious practical value. Solutions are available for special kinds of nonlinear equations, and a variety of techniques can be used to transform equations into different forms, but none of this guarantees that a solution for any given equation can be found. In nonlinear cases, it is more likely that a differential equation can be solved, simply because more work has been done in this area, but it is also true that neither differential nor difference equations can be said to have readily available solutions.

A second distinction between the two types of equations concerns the nature of the solutions. Under certain conditions, analogous pairs of difference and differential equations will exhibit very different behaviors. This can be illustrated by considering a class of equations with readily available solutions for both difference and differential equations: linear equations with constant coefficients. In the case of analogous pairs of first-order linear difference and differential equations, the same initial conditions and coefficient values can generate qualitatively different time paths. For the difference equation the possible kinds of behavior are monotonic divergence, monotonic convergence, divergence with oscillation, and convergence with oscillation. For the differential equation, the possible kinds of behavior are monotonic divergence and monotonic convergence. The equilibrium value will always be the same for analogous pairs of difference and differential equations since, by definition, the equilibrium point will be the point for which successive differences or derivatives equal zero. Thus, *the difference equation allows for a greater diversity of patterns of qualitative behavior* (Samuelson, 1974).

Second-order linear equations with constant coefficients exhibit similar patterns. As in the first-order case, two major distinctions occur: (1) difference equations are less stable, and (2) difference equations exhibit period two oscillations in addition to the behavior patterns common to both equations. This means that the same initial conditions and parameter values governing change can result in different qualitative as well as quantitative behaviors. Difference equations are generally less stable than their differential counterparts: An equation that converges in differential form may diverge in difference equation form, but the converse is not true. For nonlinear equations, conditions for the local stability of difference equations are more stringent than the ones for corresponding differential equations— the parameter space for difference equation convergence will be a subspace of the convergent parameter space of the corresponding differential equation (May, 1974: 24-30). Difference equations also exhibit a second kind of "instability" in the form of oscillatory motion instead of monotonic behavior. Technically, the term "instability" is reserved for divergent behavior, but oscillatory behavior may appear unstable in a *substantive* sense when oscillations represent large changes in a relatively short time period. Difference equations often exhibit oscillatory behavior patterns in regions that, for analogous parameters, yield a smooth pattern from the corresponding differential equation. These differences in stability conditions, both in the technical sense and in the substantive sense, arise as a consequence of the mode of formalization.

In summary, then, since the solutions of the two versions are different, it is likely that numerical time paths generated by analogous pairs of difference and differential equations will differ. Furthermore, local stability conditions for difference equations are more stringent than those for analogous differential equations. This conclusion would also appear to be true of global stability conditions, where such conditions exist and are known. Finally, for some parameter values, analogous pairs of difference and differential equations will generate different qualitative patterns of behavior even when stability conditions are satisfied for both equations. (For a more complete discussion of the differences between analogous pairs of difference and differential equations see Kohfeld and Salert, 1982.)

NOTES

1. For treatments of difference equations see Samuelson (1974), Baumol (1970), Goldberg (1958), Cadzow (1973), and Boynton (1980).

2. This distinction between diachronic and synchronic change relies upon a discussion contained in Cortes et al. (1974: ch. 1).

3. Period two oscillation is the most basic oscillatory pattern in which positive and negative rates of change alternate in each time period: An increase is followed by a decrease is followed by an increase and so on.

92

4. At first inspection these mobilization levels may appear somewhat low. Only 54% of the population is susceptible to Democratic party recruitment efforts, and the process converges toward an equilibrium of only 37% Democratic party support. The level of mobilization, however, is defined to the base of all eligibles rather than to all voters. The mean Lake County turnout rate for presidential elections from 1956 to 1968 was approximately 69%. Using this figure as a norm, the pool of potential recruits is 78% of average turnout, and the mobilization equilibrium is 54% of average turnout. Thus, rather than indicating weakness, this analysis points to the strength of the Democratic party in Lake County.

5. We are pursuing a solution strategy that relies on the work of Goldberg (1958). For a useful, compressed outline see Cortes et al. (1974). The strategy developed here is one of several for solving difference equations. One alternative approach—the z-transform—is set forth in Cadzow (1973). See the Appendix for illustrations of recursive form, canonical form, and homogeneous form difference equations.

6. Readers unfamiliar with complex numbers might find it beneficial to consult a college algebra text.

7. We follow Richardson's convention of assuming that all parameters are positive, and several later results depend upon this assumption. It should be mentioned, however, that it is at least plausible that some parameters might be negative, and some investigators allow for that possibility.

8. A single higher-order linear difference equation can be expressed as a system of first-order linear difference equations. By defining an additional system state (Z_t), the reader should be persuaded that an alternative form for equation 4.53 is:

$$A_t = -Z_{t-1} + \alpha U_t$$

$$Z_t = \beta A_{t-1}$$

Indeed, one general formulation of the feedback model isolates feedback as a separate, unobservable system state (isolated in a separate auxiliary equation) that is eliminated when the system is put into a reduced form (Boynton, 1980: 139).

9. Time delays in feedback are destabilizing in the most general sense as well. Higher-order lag structures produce a greater number of roots, thereby increasing the likelihood that one of the roots will exceed limits on stability.

10. The statistical procedures typically utilized in these empirical analyses have been criticized by Hibbs (1974) as producing biased, inconsistent estimates, and artificially inflated tests of significance. The problem stems from serially correlated error terms in the time series as a result of lagging endogenous variables on the right-hand side of the estimating equation.

11. In more complex nonlinear equations, especially when written in discrete time, it is possible for the graph technique presented here to break down, since trajectories can "jump over" equilibrium lines from one point in time to the next. The modeler should, therefore, carefully examine the possible range of acceptable parameter values when using these methods.

REFERENCES

ALLEN, R.G.D. (1963) Mathematical Economics. London: Macmillan.
BARTHOLOMEW, D. J. (1967) Stochastic Models for Social Processes. Cambridge: Cambridge University Press.
BAUMOL, W. J. (1970) Economic Dynamics. London: Collier-Macmillan.
BERELSON, B. R., P. F. LAZARSFELD, and W. N. McPHEE (1954) Voting. Chicago: University of Chicago Press.

BOUDON, R. (1974) Education, Opportunity, and Social Inequality. New York: John Wiley.

BOYNTON, G. R. (1980) Mathematical Thinking about Politics. New York: Longman.

BRAND, L. (1966) Differential and Difference Equations. New York: John Wiley.

BRUNNER, R. D. and G. D. BREWER (1971) Organized Complexity: Empirical Theories of Political Development. New York: Macmillan.

BURNHAM, W. D. (1970) Critical Elections and the Mainsprings of American Politics. New York: W. W. Norton.

CADZOW, J. A. (1973) Discrete Time Systems: An Introduction with Interdisplinary Applications. Englewood Cliffs, NJ: Prentice-Hall.

CHAUNDY, T. W. and E. PHILLIPS (1936) "The convergence of sequences defined by quadratic recurrence formulae." Quarterly Journal of Mathematics, Oxford Series: 74-80.

CHORLTON, F. (1965) Ordinary Differential and Difference Equations: Theory and Applications. New York: Van Nostrand.

CHURCHILL, R. V. (1972) Operational Mathematics. New York: McGraw-Hill.

COLEMAN, J S. (1964) Introduction to Mathematical Sociology. New York: Macmillan.

CORTES, F., A. PRZEWORSKI, and J. SPRAGUE (1974) Systems Analysis for Social Scientists. New York: John Wiley.

DAVIS, O. A., M.A.H. DEMPSTER, and A. WILDAVSKY (1966) "A theory of the budgetary process." American Political Science Review 60 (September): 529-547.

DURKHEIM, E. (1951) [1897] Suicide. New York: Macmillan.

ERBRING, L. (1975) "The impact of political events on mass publics: public opinion dynamics and an approach to dynamic analysis." Ph.D. dissertation, University of Michigan.

FENNO, R. F., Jr. (1966) The Power of the Purse. Boston: Little, Brown.

FEREJOHN, J. and R. NOLL (1978) "Uncertainty and the formal theory of political campaigns." American Political Science Review 72: 492-505.

GILLESPIE, J V. and D. A. ZINNES [eds.] (1977) Mathematical Systems in International Relations Research. New York: Praeger.

GOLDBERG, S. (1958) Difference Equations. New York: John Wiley.

GOSNELL, H. F. (1927) Getting Out the Vote: An Experiment in the Stimulation of Voting. Chicago: University of Chicago Press.

HAMMING, R. W. (1971) Introduction to Applied Numerical Analysis. New York: McGraw-Hill.

HIBBS, D. A., Jr. (1976) "Industrial conflict in advanced industrial societies." American Political Science Review 70 (December): 1033-1058.

——— (1974) "Problems of statistical estimation and causal inference in time-series models," pp. 252-308 in H. L. Costner (ed.) Sociological Methodology 1973-1974. San Francisco: Jossey-Bass.

HIRSCH, M. W. and S. SMALE (1974) Differential Equations, Dynamical Systems and Linear Algebra. New York: Academic.

HUCKFELDT, R. R. (1982a) "Social contexts, social networks, and political influence." Working Paper. Notre Dame, IN: University of Notre Dame.

——— (1982b) "Political influence and the social context: is stability the source of volatility?" Working Paper. Notre Dame, IN: University of Notre Dame.

——— (1981) The Dynamics of Political Mobilization: I and II. UMAP Modules 297 and 298. Boston: Education Development Center by Birkhauser.

——— (1980) "Variable responses to neighborhood social contexts: assimilation, conflict, and tipping points." Political Behavior 2: 231-258.

——— (1979) "Political participation and the neighborhood social context." American Journal of Political Science 23 (August): 579-592.

JOHNSEN, C. (1978) "Urban investment and municipal expenditures." Working Paper. St. Louis, MO: Washington University.

94

KOHFELD, C. W. (1981) "Soft data, the policy process, and qualitative dynamics." Political Methodology 7: 27-42.

——— (1979) The Growth of Partisan Support II: Model and Analytics. UMAP Module No. 305. Newton, MA: Educational Development Center.

——— (1976) "Conflict and policy dynamics in the local community." Ph.D. dissertation. Washington University, St. Louis, MO.

——— and T. W. LIKENS (1982) "Mass compliance and social interaction: a dynamic formulation." Law & Policy Quarterly 3 (July).

KOHFELD, C. W. and B. SALERT (1982) "Discrete and continuous representation of dynamic models." Political Methodology 8.

La PORTE, T. R. [ed.] (1975) Organized Social Complexity. Princeton, NJ: Princeton University Press.

LASSWELL, H. D. (1958) Politics: Who Gets What, When and How. New York: Meridian.

LEWIS-BECK, M. and J. ALFORD (1980) "Can government regulate safety? the coal mine example." American Political Science Review 74 (September): 745-756.

LIKENS, T. W. (1979) The Budgetary Process: Competition. UMAP Module No. 333. Newton, MA: Educational Development Center.

——— (1978) "Dynamic processes in politics: theoretical principles and strategies of research." Ph.D. dissertation, Washington University, St. Louis, MO

——— and C. W. KOHFELD (1980) "Models of Mass Compliance: Contextual or Economic Approach?" Presented at American Political Science Convention, Washington, D.C.

MacKUEN, M. (1981) "Social communication and the mass policy agenda," in M. MacKuen and S. Coombs (eds.) More than News: Media Power in Public Affairs. Beverly Hills, CA: Sage.

MAY, R. M. (1974) Stability and Complexity in Model Ecosystems. Princeton, NJ: Princeton University Press.

McCLEARY, R. and R. A. HAY, Jr. (1980) Applied Time Series Analysis for the Social Sciences. Beverly Hills, CA: Sage.

McPHEE, W. N. (1963) Formal Theories of Mass Behavior. New York: Macmillan.

OSTROM, C. W., Jr. (1978) Time Series Analysis: Regression Techniques. Sage University Paper on Quantitative Applications in the Social Sciences No. 07-009. Bevery Hills, CA: Sage.

PRZEWORSKI, A. (1975) "Institutionalization of voting patterns or is mobilization the source of decay?" American Political Science Review 69 (March): 49-67.

——— and J. SPRAGUE (1978) "Class mobilization in selected Western European political systems." Presented at the Annual Meetings of the American Political Science Association, New York, August 30-September 3.

QUINE, W.O.V. (1961) From a Logical Point of View. New York: Harper & Row.

RAPOPORT, A. (1963) "Mathematical models of social interaction," in R. D. Luce (ed.) Handbook of Mathematical Psychology, Vol. 2. New York: John Wiley.

RICHARDSON, L. F. (1960) Arms and Insecurity. Pittsburgh: Boxwood.

RITGER, P. D. and N. J. ROSE (1968) Differential Equations with Applications. New York: McGraw-Hill.

ROSEN, R. (1970) Dynamical System Theory in Biology, Vol. 1. Stability Theory and Its Application. New York: John Wiley.

SAMUELSON, P. A. (1974) [1947] Foundations of Economic Analysis. New York: Atheneum.

SCHELLING, T. C. (1978) Micromotives and Macrobehavior. New York: W. W. Norton.

SCHRODT, P. A. and M. D. WARD (1981) "Statistical inference in incremental and difference equation models." American Journal of Political Science 25 (November): 815-832.

SHARKANSKY, I. (1968) "Agency requests, gubernatorial support and budget success in state legislatures." American Political Science Review 62 (December): 1220-1231.

———— (1965) "Four agencies and an appropriations subcommittee." Midwest Journal of Political Science 9 (August): 254-281.

SIMON, H. A. (1957) Models of Man. New York: Wiley and Sons.

SPRAGUE, J. (1981) "One-party dominance in legislatures." Legislative Studies Quarterly 6: 259-285.

———— (1980) "Two variants of aggregation processes and problems in elementary dynamic and contextual causal formulations." Political Science Paper No. 50. St. Louis, MO: Washington University.

———— (1980a) "A priori requirements on descriptive political theory." Political Science Paper No. 47. St. Louis, MO: Washington University.

———— (1980b) "On Duverger's sociological law: the connection between electoral laws and party systems." Political Science Paper No. 48. St. Louis, MO: Washington University.

———— (1976) "Comments on mobilization processes represented as difference equations or difference equation systems." Working Paper. St. Louis, MO: Washington University.

———— (1976) "Discrete linear systems as useful models for political analysis: three applications." Presented at the Annual Meeting of the Society for General Systems Research, Boston, MA, February.

———— (1975) "Democrats as predacious do-gooders: a study of the interdependence of public problems, public policies, and politics." Presented at the the Annual Meeting of the Public Choice Society, Chicago, April 3-5.

———— (1973) "Three applications of contextual theses: cross section, across time, and across parameters." Working Paper. St. Louis, MO: Washington University.

———— (1969) "A nonlinear difference equation." Working Paper. St. Louis, MO: Washington University.

TUFTE, E. R. (1978) Political Control of the Economy. Princeton, NJ: Princeton University Press.

WILDAVSKY, A. (1979) The Politics of the Budgetary Process. Boston: Little, Brown.

———— (1975) Budgeting: A Comparative Theory of the Budgetary Process. Boston: Little, Brown.

R. ROBERT HUCKFELDT is Assistant Professor of Government at the University of Notre Dame. He is author of several articles dealing with politics and the social context. He is currently engaged in a research project concerned with political assimilation and conflict in urban contexts.

C. W. KOHFELD is Assistant Professor of Political Science and Fellow in the Center for Metropolitan Studies at the University of Missouri—St. Louis. She received her Ph.D. from Washington University in St. Louis in 1976. She is the author of several articles, the most recent of which, coauthored with T. W. Likens, is "Mass Compliance and Social Interaction: a Dynamic Formulation" in Law & Policy Quarterly *(July 1982).*

THOMAS W. LIKENS is currently Manager of Industry and Government Planning for the Anheuser-Busch Companies in St. Louis. He is formerly Assistant Professor of Political Science at the University of Kentucky and Visiting Research Professor at the University of Denver. His research interests include mathematical modeling, mass behavior, and policy analysis.

Printed in the United States
98554LV00002B/37/A

28856661R00061

Printed in Great Britain
by Amazon